OPEN THE GIFT

Discovering the Treasures God Gave Us
When He Gave Us Jesus

Sheila Alewine
www.aroundthecornerministries.org

Around The Corner Ministries exists to take the gospel to every neighborhood in America. Our mission is to equip followers of Jesus to engage their neighborhoods and communities with the gospel of Jesus Christ.

ISBN: 978-1-7330478-6-9

If we seek salvation, we are taught by the very name of Jesus that it is of Him.
If we seek any other gifts of the Spirit, they will be found in His anointing.
If we seek strength, it lies in His dominion;
if purity, in His conception;
if gentleness, it appears in His birth.
For by His birth He was made like us in all respects, that He might learn to feel our pain.
If we seek redemption, it lies in His passion;
if acquittal, in His condemnation;
if remission of the curse, in His cross;
if satisfaction, in His sacrifice;
if purification, in His blood;
if reconciliation, in His descent into hell;
if mortification of the flesh, in His tomb;
if newness of life, in His resurrection;
if immortality, in the same;
if inheritance of the Heavenly Kingdom, in His entrance into heaven;
if protection, if security, if abundant supply of all blessings, in His Kingdom;
if untroubled expectation of judgment, in the power given to Him to judge.
In short, since rich store of every kind of good abounds in Him,
let us drink our fill from this fountain,
and from no other.
—John Calvin

CONTENTS

Salvation Gifts

Day 1-7

> Reconciliation, Justification, A New Life, Faith, Repentance, Grace, Mercy

Sanctifying Gifts

Day 8-14

> Truth, Conviction, Victory, Forgiveness, The Mind of Christ, Weakness, Holiness

Satisfying Gifts

Day 15-18

> Abundant Life, Family, Friendship, Inheritance

Serving Gifts

Day 19-24

> Spiritual Gifts, Purpose, Kingdom, Fruit, Help, Wisdom

Strengthening Gifts

Day 25-29

> Holy Spirit, Security, Courage, Trials, Prayer

Sustaining Gifts

Day 30-36

> Provision, Rest, Peace, Hope, Love, Joy, Comfort

Spectacular Gifts

Day 37-40

> Covenant, Immortality, Rewards, Heaven

A Word To The Reader

For God so loved the world,
that He gave His only begotten Son,
that whoever believes in Him shall not perish,
but have eternal life.
John 3:16

Christmas is the time when we celebrate the arrival of the tiny baby that came from heaven, His birth announced by an angelic choir and marked with a bright star that led wise men to worship. Born to simple people and raised in a small village where surely everyone knew Him to be a kind, wise, and mature-beyond-His-age young man, He lived just thirty-three short years. To the surprise of many, He became a rebel in the religious culture of His day and was executed by those who claimed to speak for God.

We know the real story. Jesus was the only begotten Son of God, sent to purchase our salvation and rescue us from the sin that separated us from our Creator. He came to give us the gift of eternal, abundant life today, and the promise of a glorified life in His presence when we say goodbye to this world.

I believe those who have placed their faith in Jesus have the potential to experience soul-satisfying joy and contentment in every circumstance. In Him, we have received an unending treasure that meets every need, overcomes every sin, soothes every hurt, and gives every trial a purpose that outweighs the burden of its pain. Even so, as true Christ-followers, we can find ourselves in seasons of discouragement or depression. Our flesh is susceptible to being captured by addictive behaviors; we may be lonely or struggle with antisocial tendencies. We may at times feel powerless and ill-equipped to serve in our local church, make an impact for God's kingdom, or simply to get through our day-to-day obligations with some semblance of emotional and spiritual well-being.

While those in Christ may encounter places of disappointments and struggle just as the rest of the world, we are not destined to live there. We have a solution. Jesus came to give us the source of all the joy and contentment we can never find without Him. He came to give us *Himself.*

Here are the questions we must answer.

Have we failed to open the gifts that Jesus brings?
Have we underestimated what He came to do?

Perhaps you're still weighing in on whether or not this Jesus is who He says He is. You don't quite see what your Christian friends are talking about; it all seems a bit foolish and unnecessary to you. And, you feel you're doing pretty well at the helm of your own life. If that's your story, then I challenge you to unlock the door to your heart as you read this book. Be honest. Be real. Ask God to show you if these words are true. My prayer is for your eyes to be opened and your heart to understand that Jesus is far better and greater and more relevant to you than you ever dreamed.

God didn't create us to flounder around in life, figuring it out as we go and attempting to either make the best of our failures or pretending they never happened. His desire is for each of us to see the truth about ourselves and recognize the empty places that will never be filled outside of Jesus. He longs to give purpose and meaning to our days and fill up our souls with real joy and peace, and a thousand other little blessings we can only imagine.

And so, He gave us Jesus.

I invite you to open the gift. We begin our journey with salvation and all it provides and will end in the throne room of heaven. I'm praying that, along the way, God will reveal to us just how much He gave us when He gave us Jesus.

Thanks for taking this journey with me,

Sheila Alewine
October 1, 2020

SALVATION GIFTS
Day 1 – Day 7

And there is salvation in no one else;
for there is no other name under heaven
that has been given among men
by which we must be saved.
Acts 4:12

Jesus came to give us salvation.
He has reconciled us to the Father and declared us to be righteous,
justified in the Father's eyes only because we stand in Him.
In grace and mercy, He granted us repentance and gave us faith to believe.
Salvation is the gift of a brand-new life unlike anything we've ever known.

DAY 1: THE GIFT OF RECONCILIATION

*The glorious good news of the gospel is that the sin-devastated relationship
between lost sinners and the holy God can be restored.
But through God's plan of reconciliation all the hostility, animosity,
and alienation separating the Holy One and sinners vanishes,
and those who were once His enemies become His friends.*
–John MacArthur[1]

Romans 5:8-11 – *But God demonstrates His own love toward us, in that while we
were yet sinners, Christ died for us. Much more then, having now been justified by
His blood, we shall be saved from the wrath of God through Him. For if while we
were enemies we were reconciled to God through the death of His Son, much more,
having been reconciled, we shall be saved by His life. And not only this, but we also
exult in God through our Lord Jesus Christ, through whom we have now received
the reconciliation.*

God sent Jesus right into His enemy's camp. We don't normally think of the
Christmas story as a war story, but at its heart, it was a rescue mission. God sent
His best and bravest soldier into enemy territory as a newborn, red, wrinkled
infant. It would take the power of God to destroy the enemy; a surprise attack
was necessary. No one expected deliverance and freedom to come in the form of
a tiny baby.

To understand the magnitude of God's gift, we have to first know we are His
enemies. There's a dividing wall between a holy God and sinful men. Paul called
it "the enmity" when he spoke about the law of God that calls us to account for
our sinful deeds. We are born into it, broken people, a fallen nature inherited
from our ancestor, Adam. We begin our own lives as squalling, needy children,
born into the camp of lost souls, bound in the dominion of darkness.

Colossians 1:13-14 – *For He rescued us from the domain of darkness, and
transferred us to the kingdom of His beloved Son, in whom we have redemption,
the forgiveness of sins.*

We need to be reconciled to our Creator, to be brought back into favor with
Him. We are at odds with Him not only because of our inherited sin nature,
but as a result of our own willful, sinful deeds. This is not a case of both
parties being wrong and coming to a compromise so that the relationship
can be restored. All the fault is on us, and without God acting on our behalf,
we can never be reconciled to Him.

The word *reconciliation* does mean to "return to favor" but also has the deeper meaning of an exchange. When you reconcile your checkbook, you balance both the debits and credits. They must equal out for your bank account to reconcile.

Jesus came to reconcile our accounts with God. We owed a debt we could not pay, a sin debt, that could only be accounted for by our death. And even then, our physical death could never make us holy and righteous; we would still have a spiritual deficit. We could not bribe our way out of the enemy's camp.

God reconciles us *in Christ.* He makes an exchange. When Christ died, He took our sin to His account and in exchange, gave us His righteousness. We are brought back into favor with God.

We are reconciled.

The first step to know Christ is to know ourselves. We must recognize that we are enemies of God until we receive the gift of reconciliation.

What is the first thing a person does when he has been rescued from an enemy? *He looks behind him to see who else needs rescuing!* When a prisoner of war hears the sound of troops coming to set him free, he runs toward his rescuers to gain his own freedom. When he realizes the enemy has no more authority to harm or hold him, he will immediately bring all the influence and power of those who rescued him to set his fellow prisoners free.

2 Corinthians 5:18-20 – *Now all these things are from God, who reconciled us to Himself through Christ and gave us the ministry of reconciliation, namely, that God was in Christ reconciling the world to Himself, not counting their trespasses against them, and He has committed to us the word of reconciliation. Therefore, we are ambassadors for Christ, as though God were making an appeal through us; we beg you on behalf of Christ, be reconciled to God.*

Have you received the gift of reconciliation in Jesus? If so, rejoice! You are a favored child of God. Now, look behind you and see who else needs rescuing!

Pray Today

Dear Jesus, Thank You for reconciling me to the Father. You came into our world knowing it would hate You, persecute You, and ultimately kill You. You gave up Your life so that I could be brought back into favor with God, having all my sinful accounts cancelled out in exchange for Your righteousness. You reconciled me while I was still your enemy, and now I am called to tell others about this great gift available to them. Thank You for the gift of reconciliation. Amen.

DAY 2: THE GIFT OF JUSTIFICATION

This is the rock where we stand when the dark clouds gather and the floods
lick at our feet: justification is by grace alone (not mixed with our merit),
through faith alone (not mixed with our works)
on the basis of Christ alone (not mingling his righteousness with ours),
to the glory of God alone (not ours).

—John Piper[2]

Romans 3:21-26 – *But now apart from the Law the righteousness of God has been manifested, being witnessed by the Law and the Prophets, even the righteousness of God through faith in Jesus Christ for all those who believe; for there is no distinction; for all have sinned and fall short of the glory of God, being justified as a gift by His grace through the redemption which is in Christ Jesus; whom God displayed publicly as a propitiation in His blood through faith. This was to demonstrate His righteousness, because in the forbearance of God He passed over the sins previously committed; for the demonstration, I say, of His righteousness at the present time, so that He would be just and the justifier of the one who has faith in Jesus.*

A common argument against the Bible's teaching that Jesus is the only way to salvation is that it is unfair. Why should we believe in a God that says His way is the only way? Is this a God who is loving? How fair is it that only those "Christians" who believe a certain way are the ones who get into heaven?

The argument is flawed, because it makes the assumption that Christ-followers are allowed into heaven because they believe. This is not true. Believing, no matter how deep or passionate our faith is, does not accomplish what is required for entrance into God's eternal kingdom. If it did, it would be a religion based on works, just like every other false religion.

We cannot *believe* our way into heaven; we must be *made righteous*. We must be *justified* before God, something we cannot achieve by our own efforts.

Justification is a big word that simply means to be made right. When God justifies us, He declares that we are righteous, or right with Him, and thus welcomed into heaven. Heaven is a place where sin cannot abide. God is holy. He illustrated His holiness in the strict laws of sacrifice and atonement by which His people, the Israelites, were to abide. Failure to follow God's sacrificial statutes resulted in instant death in many cases.

As sinful human beings, born with a fallen nature inherited from Adam, the only way we can be made righteous in God's eyes is if He looks at us in Christ's righteousness. Christ's death on the cross accomplished our justification, and it is given as a gift, never earned by our belief or by our good works.

God took our sin and placed it on His Son, Jesus. Jesus paid the penalty for us.

Romans 6:23 – *For the wages of sin is death, but the free gift of God is eternal life in Christ Jesus our Lord.*

Sin requires a sacrifice; something has to die to atone for it. This is how God could declare the Old Testament saints righteous. He passed over their sins until the time when Jesus paid the debt. Their sacrifice of lambs, goats, and bulls was an act of obedience, looking forward to the future Lamb of God who would take away the sin of the world (John 1:29).

God never excuses our sin. Sin always requires a payment, and this payment comes in the form a gift – the gift of justification. We are made righteous only by the atoning act of Jesus on the cross. Belief is necessary, not to justify ourselves before God, but to access and receive the gift that has already been offered on our behalf. Belief is a response to what God has already done.

Scripture warns us that all of us will stand before God and give account for our lives. What relief! What joy! What assurance we have that because of Christ, we can stand and be counted as righteous because we have received the gift of justification! Jesus came to make us righteous and give us the hope of eternal life. In gratitude, let's live as the holy people Christ has made us to be.

Titus 3:5-7 – *He saved us, not on the basis of deeds which we have done in righteousness, but according to His mercy, by the washing of regeneration and renewing by the Holy Spirit, whom He poured out upon us richly through Jesus Christ our Savior, so that being justified by His grace we would be made heirs according to the hope of eternal life.*

Pray Today

Dear Jesus, Thank you for the gift of justification. How fearful it would be to stand before You in all Your holiness, and only then recognize the reality of our sinful state. We're so thankful that You came so that we could be made righteous. You took our sin on Yourself and graciously exchanged it for Your righteousness, making us acceptable to the Father and granting us entrance into Your kingdom, and the eternal joy and glory of heaven. Remind us daily to walk in the righteousness that You have gifted to us and help us tell those around us that they, too, can be justified by grace, through repentance and faith in You. Amen.

DAY 3: THE GIFT OF A NEW LIFE

The new birth is no mere turning over a new leaf,
but is the inception and reception of a new life.
It is no mere reformation but a complete transformation.
In short, the new birth is a miracle,
the result of the supernatural operation of God.
It is radical, revolutionary, lasting.
—A.W. Pink[3]

2 Corinthians 5:17 – *Therefore if anyone is in Christ, he is a new creature; the old things passed away; behold, new things have come.*

A common desire among human beings is the longing for something new. A new year, a new beginning, a fresh start. As a child, we looked forward to the excitement of a new school year; we went "school shopping" for new clothes, new shoes, new supplies. I loved (and still love) opening a new notebook, unspoiled and waiting for inspiration. As adults, we are constantly trading up (or trading in) for something different, something new, whether it's a car, a house, or a job.

I believe this longing for "something new" is a by-product of our fallen nature. We inherently sense there's something missing, something more. Thanks be to God for the day we realized that nothing in this world would ever satisfy that longing.

Jesus gives us the ultimate gift of a new life, a new beginning when we come to Him by faith and receive salvation. Paul describes those in Christ as "new creatures," a phrase which immediately takes us back to Genesis when God first created man and woman. Adam and Eve were created by God, perfect, holy, and blameless, innocent, and unaware of sin until they disobeyed and broke God's command. This brokenness, this fallen nature, would be passed down to every human being, and with it, an awareness and constant desire to be re-created anew.

In Christ, we are *made new*. The Greek word translated "new" is *kainos* and denotes not another of the same kind, but new in form and quality and nature. God literally recreates us in salvation, restoring us back to the original image of God. We have a new perspective, new desires, and a new source of power to live through the indwelling Spirit of God.

We have a new life.

As exciting and wonderful as the new life is, equally as exciting is the promise that the old life passes away. Have you ever visited the eye doctor because you realized your vision was blurry? He explains to you that you need a new prescription to see things clearly and sends you home with a new pair of glasses. How helpful would it be to continue to wear your old glasses and tuck the new pair away in a drawer to save for the future?

Perhaps you have a favorite pair of boots that you are unwilling to give up, even though the soles are worn and you find your socks wet and your feet cold every time you venture out in them. You've already purchased a new pair, but you're saving them for when you "really need them."

Sadly, this is what many of us do as new creations in Christ. We continue to live the old life when God has made us new creatures and given us a new life. He has done the work spiritually; we are *made new.* He has turned on the light for us spiritually; we have to decide whether we want to walk in that light, or stumble around in the darkness with blurry vision, unprotected from what we might walk into! The new life Jesus came to give us starts *now.*

What are you holding onto from your old life that needs to be laid aside so that you can enjoy the new life God has given you? Are there habits or sins that need to be confessed and abandoned? Is your value system and worldview based on scripture or your own knowledge and perspective from the world's culture? Is your time and talent dedicated to the new call God has on your life, or are you still working for your own glory and success?

Jesus came to give us the gift of a new life. Let me say it again. *We have a new life.* Let's not waste a moment more in the old one.

Romans 6:4 – *Therefore we have been buried with Him through baptism into death, so that as Christ was raised from the dead through the glory of the Father, so we too might walk in newness of life.*

Pray Today

Dear Jesus, Thank you for the gift of a new life. You have made us a new creation. Thank you that our old life has passed away and we have the opportunity and ability to enjoy the new life You made possible by Your death and resurrection. We recognize that You are making all things new, restoring what sin stole from Your creation. Help us to walk in newness of life and abandon all that would keep us rooted in our old ways of living without You. Amen.

DAY 4: THE GIFT OF FAITH

> We must never think of salvation as a kind of transaction between God
> and us in which He contributes grace and we contribute faith.
> For we were dead and had to be quickened before we could believe.
> No, Christ's apostles clearly teach elsewhere that saving faith too is
> God's gracious gift.
> —John Stott[4]

Ephesians 2:8 – *For by grace you have been saved through faith; and that not of yourselves, it is the gift of God; not as a result of works, so that no one may boast.*

Hebrews 11:1-2,6 – *Now faith is the assurance of things hoped for, the conviction of things not seen. For by it men of old gained approval. And without faith it is impossible to please Him, for he who comes to God must believe that he is and that He is a rewarder of those who seek Him.*

Have you ever thought about the source of your faith? Faith is a requirement for salvation. I must take God at His word, and by faith, place my full confidence and trust in the finished work of Jesus. I believe in something that, in my human understanding, seems unbelievable.

The word translated *faith* in the New Testament is *pistis*; the root word means "to persuade." Faith is a firm persuasion based on hearing. It is a firm conviction that something is true, so much so, that we entrust our lives to it.

Romans 10:17 – *So faith comes from hearing, and hearing by the word of Christ.*

Who persuaded you? Who convinced you that the gospel is true, that you were born into sin and separated from God? How did you come to understand and believe that Jesus is the only way to be saved?

God had to give you faith. His Spirit spoke to you and revealed truth to you. He gave you faith as a gift, so that you could believe and receive salvation. In order to have faith in God, you first had to hear with your ears, but you also had to hear and understand with your heart. And only God can speak to the heart.

Romans 12:3 – *For through the grace given to me I say to everyone among you not to think more highly of himself than he ought to think; but to think so as to have sound judgment, as God has allotted to each a measure of faith.*

Faith in God is an amazing thing. It is alive. It's not some sterile, stagnant, academic ideology found in dusty books. It's not a set of rules and regulations by which humans control each other to adhere to cultic behaviors. No, faith is a living, changing, growing relationship with the divine Creator. Saving faith starts as a tiny mustard seed planted in our hearts by the Holy Spirit to reveal that God loves us and sent His Son to Calvary to pay our sin debt and provide a way back into His holy and righteous favor. That tiny seed of faith must be watered and nourished by daily submission and obedience to the object of our faith, Jesus. Then it will send its roots down deep to keep us anchored in truth, all the while spreading outward and upward into a life that honors and glorifies God, as *we walk by faith not by sight* (2 Corinthians 5:7).

The writer of Hebrews tells us that Jesus is both the author and perfecter of faith, as seen by His willingness to go to the cross. As the author of faith, He took the lead, setting the example for us. He is the original, the primary, the standard in faithful obedience; He shows us what it means to exercise faith. As the perfecter of faith, He is the finisher, the completer. He set the highest standard by completing His mission, and God honored and accepted His faithful act of sacrifice by raising Him up from the grave and seating Him at His right hand (Philippians 2:5-11; Colossians 3:1).

This is the kind of faith God has given us if we will accept and exercise it. We are to fix our eyes on Jesus. He alone is to be the object of our faith, the example of our faith, and the source of our faith. God begins His work in us by granting us a measure of faith to believe in Him, and He continues His work by growing our faith until the day He takes us home and our faith becomes sight.

Faith is not *your* work, but *God's* work in you, a gift He planned long ago when He gave us Jesus.

Hebrews 12:1-2 – *Therefore, since we have so great a cloud of witnesses surrounding us, let us also lay aside every encumbrance and the sin which so easily entangles us, and let us run with endurance the race that is set before us, fixing our eyes on Jesus, the author and perfecter of faith, who for the joy set before Him endured the cross, despising the shame, and has sat down at the right hand of the throne of God.*

Pray Today

Dear Jesus, Thank you for the gift of faith. You made a way for me to hear the good news of the gospel, and Your Holy Spirit convinced and persuaded me that it was indeed true. You gave me faith to believe in You. Help me to walk by faith. Give me patient endurance as You grow my faith. May I be a faithful and obedient servant in gratitude for Your gift until my faith becomes sight. Amen.

DAY 5: THE GIFT OF REPENTANCE

There can be no repentance or faith until the heart has been re-created.
But in the moment of regeneration, the Holy Spirit imparts the gift
of repentant faith to sinners – bringing them to saving faith in Christ
and enabling them to turn away from sin.
The result is a dramatic conversion.
–John MacArthur[5]

2 Timothy 2:24-26 – *The Lord's bond-servant must not be quarrelsome, but be kind to all, able to teach, patient when wronged, with gentleness correcting those who are in opposition, if perhaps God may grant them repentance leading to the knowledge of the truth, and they may come to their senses and escape from the snare of the devil, having been held captive by him to do his will.*

Faith and repentance are two distinct elements of salvation, but they are inextricably linked. We cannot exercise true faith in Christ for the forgiveness of our sins without first repenting of those sins. It's simply not possible.

Repentance is a change of mind, a turning away. It is to recognize the futility of human thought that has resulted in our sinful actions and attitudes and intentionally turn towards God. Repentance involves confession, which is to say, we agree with God about our sin and by faith call out to Him for forgiveness and reconciliation.

Repentance involves more than regret. We regret things because we don't like the consequences of our choices, but regret must lead to true repentance. This is why repentance is a gift. God commands us to repent and believe, but unless He shows us the reality of our sinful condition, we will never turn away from it and respond with faith in Him.

How is repentance a gift? Isn't it simply an act of our will? God does not force anyone but according to scripture, He provides both the *time* and the *motivation* to respond to His command to repent.

God extends patience to give time for repentance.

Romans 2:4 – *Or do you think lightly of the riches of His kindness and tolerance and patience, not knowing that the kindness of God leads you to repentance?*

2 Peter 3:9 – *The Lord is not slow about His promise, as some count slowness, but is patient toward you, not wishing for any to perish but for all to come to repentance.*

What if we received the immediate consequences of our sin? None of us would live past the age of five! The wages of sin is death, yet God is so gracious, He withholds our punishment in light of Christ's substitutionary atonement on the cross. He woos us. He draws us. He protects us from the consequences of our poor choices. He is tolerant and kind and patient, allowing us time to come to our senses and turn away from sin.

God allows pain to give motivation for repentance.

2 Corinthians 7:9-10 – *I now rejoice, not that you were made sorrowful, but that you were made sorrowful to the point of repentance; for you were made sorrowful according to the will of God, so that you might not suffer loss in anything through us. For the sorrow that is according to the will of God produces a repentance without regret, leading to salvation, but the sorrow of the world produces death.*

We don't often think of pain as a gift, but godly sorrow is one of God's most gracious acts. God created the human body with thousands of pain receptors which warn us when something is physically wrong. He created our inner being with the capacity to feel pain as well, so that we know something is spiritually wrong. To be made sorrowful is to grieve or be distressed. It is the gift of this spiritual, mental, and emotional pain that motivates us for change. Sorrow over our sin that comes by the will of God produces repentance as we acknowledge the pain and grief it has caused us, and others.

Repentance is a salvation gift which we experience when we first believe, but like many of God's gifts, it keeps on giving throughout our lives as we learn to walk with God. All Christ-followers know the sorrow of disobeying God, of spiritual failures, of feeling that we've let Him down once again. How good it is to open up the gift of repentance and come back into the sweet fellowship of our patient and kind Savior, who welcomes the repentant child with open arms.

Acts 5:30-31 – *The God of our fathers raised up Jesus, whom you had put to death by hanging Him on a cross. He is the one whom God exalted to His right hand as a Prince and a Savior, to grant repentance to Israel, and forgiveness of sins.*

Pray Today

Dear Jesus, How thankful we are that You brought us to repentance. Your patience and kindness drew us when we were still sinners, offering us the gift of unburdening our soul and laying aside all the sinful words and deeds that kept us from You. You promise to meet us with forgiveness every time. Keep our hearts tender and help us to repent quickly when we fail. Amen.

DAY 6: THE GIFT OF GRACE

Through many dangers, toils and snares,
I have already come;
'Tis grace has brought me safe thus far
and grace will lead me home.
–*Amazing Grace* by John Newton

Romans 5:1-2 – *Therefore, having been justified by faith, we have peace with God through our Lord Jesus Christ, through whom also we have obtained our introduction by faith into this grace in which we stand; and we exult in hope of the glory of God.*

If there is one word in scripture that sums up God's relationship with mankind, it is *grace*. Grace, simply put, is God's good and benevolent favor; it is the unmerited and unearned blessing of His love in action. Grace has been illustrated by the acronym **G**od's **R**iches **A**t **C**hrist's **E**xpense.

The New Testament Greek word for grace is *charis*. It is rooted in the concept of joy and pleasure and has been defined as "the absolutely free expression of the loving kindness of God to men finding its only motive in the bounty and benevolence of the Giver" (Zodhiates).

Grace is God giving us something we don't deserve; we've done nothing to earn His favor – it's simply a gift that overflows out of His very character and nature. Adam and Eve were the first human recipients of grace, created (literally shaped) by the hand of God Himself and placed in a garden which provided everything they needed to exist forever in perfect relationship with God. When they sinned, as God knew they would, He did not immediately extinguish their lives and start over, hoping to create a more worthy creature. Instead, He extended grace. He removed them from the garden so they would not eat of the Tree of Life and be eternally damned in their fallen state, even placing an angel with a flaming sword to stand guard and prevent their return. Expelling them from the Garden was not punishment; it was grace. God then sacrificed an animal and clothed their nakedness and made the first promise of a coming Savior who would redeem them by grace.

We receive salvation by grace (Ephesians 2:8-9). In the verses above, Paul tells us it is through Christ we have been introduced by faith into grace, and it is in that same grace that we stand now, as believing Christ-followers. Every day is a day of experiencing the grace of God.

Jesus is full of grace, and in relationship to Him, we receive grace upon grace. He came so that the grace God promised throughout the Old Testament could be realized (John 1:14-18). God planned to be gracious to us even before He made us; it was always His intention.

2 Timothy 1:9-10 – *Who has saved us and called us with a holy calling, not according to our works, but according to His own purpose and grace which was granted us in Christ Jesus from all eternity, but now has been revealed by the appearing of our Savior Christ Jesus, who abolished death and brought life and immortality to light through the gospel.*

Everything good comes to us by the grace of God. What have you earned? What have you received by your own merit? What blessings do you deserve? You might say, "I worked hard for that," or "I made good choices that led to this."

Think again. Who made your heart and keeps it beating? Who designed your brain and causes it to work correctly? Who designed the atmosphere with the perfect balance of elements that create the breath in your lungs? Who gives strength to your hands? Where does your creativity come from? Who placed you in your family, your home, your community? Who directed your steps so that you were at the right place, at the right time? Who made your eyes, so that you can see to read, and who enlightens your mind so that you can understand?

Think again. Who protects you when you make a mistake? Who heals your wounded emotions? Who causes your bones to knit together after being broken? Who created the systems of your body that fight off infection? Who puts you back together when you make a mess of your life?

God pours out grace every day to the wicked and undeserving who fail to see the source of the goodness and beauty of their lives. Paul defines the greatest measure of grace when he writes, *For while we were still helpless, at the right time Christ died for the ungodly. But God demonstrates His own love toward us, in that while we were yet sinners, Christ died for us* (Romans 5:6,8).

All of us were helpless sinners, deserving judgment but receiving grace. How grateful we are for the gift of grace.

John 1:16 – *For of His fullness we have all received, and grace upon grace.*

Pray Today

Dear Jesus, Thank you for the gift of grace. We will never fully know or understand the measure of grace we have received in this life, but one day, when we stand before You, we will see it clearly. Every good thing comes from You, undeserved, unmerited, and often unnoticed. Forgive us when we miss the evidence of Your grace and teach us to live grace-filled lives that overflow to others. Amen.

DAY 7: THE GIFT OF MERCY

Our Savior kneels down and gazes upon the darkest acts of our lives.
But rather than recoil in horror, He reaches out in kindness and says,
'I can clean that if you want.' And from the basin of His grace,
He scoops a palm full of mercy and washes our sin.
—Max Lucado[6]

Titus 3:4-7 – *But when the kindness of God our Savior and His love for mankind appeared, He saved us, not on the basis of deeds which we have done in righteousness, but according to His mercy, by the washing of regeneration and renewing by the Holy Spirit, whom He poured out on us richly through Jesus Christ our Savior, so that being justified by His grace we would be made heirs according to the hope of eternal life.*

Grace is God's way of dealing with our guilt through the forgiveness of sin; He provides what we can never earn (atonement). Mercy is God's way of dealing with the misery caused by our sin. He withholds what we deserve (judgment), having placed our judgment on Christ, and acts to remove the effects of sin.

We are washed.
We are regenerated.
We are renewed.

Ephesians 2:4-5 – *But God, being rich in mercy, because of His great love with which He loved us, even when we were dead in our transgressions, made us alive together with Christ (by grace you have been saved).*

Mercy is akin to compassion; pity sees the need but compassion acts to relieve the burden. God's merciful nature is moved by His love and kindness to alleviate the suffering of His creatures.

Grace and mercy are complementary expressions of God's heart for His people. God rescues us from the consequences and suffering that is our rightful due (mercy), and then blesses us and shows us favor (grace). In the courtroom of the Father, mercy steps in and takes our place as the defendant; our record is wiped clean as Jesus is sentenced for our wrongs by the Righteous Judge. Grace takes us out of the courtroom, buys us a new set of clothes, gives us a job, a place to live, and invites us over for dinner.

Salvation introduces us to the mercy of God, but this is only the beginning. God invites us to draw on His mercy daily as we navigate life as a believer. Jesus is our High Priest who continually makes intercession for us and understands that in our flesh, we are weak and frail. When trials and tribulations and the world's temptations bear down on us, stealing our peace and causing us to despair of life, we are told to draw near to God's throne of grace in full confidence of how we will be received by our God, who is *rich in mercy.*

Hebrews 4:15-16 – *For we do not have a high priest who cannot sympathize with our weaknesses, but One who has been tempted in all things as we are, yet without sin. Therefore let us draw near with confidence to the throne of grace, so that we may receive mercy and find grace to help in time of need.*

What are you facing? Physical pain? Emotional distress? Mental and spiritual attacks? Jesus experienced them all. He offers far more than sympathy or pity. He can empathize; He's been where we are, and He feels what we feel. He has compassion; He is moved to act to relieve our suffering. When we kneel at His throne and cast ourselves at His feet, we find exactly what we need: *mercy.*

The gift of mercy provides hope for the future. We can rest in the knowledge that God's heart is *for us*, that He is willing and able to rescue us when we fall. God's mercy is always timely. Though He may allow suffering to continue for a season so that our hearts can be shaped into His likeness, His mercies will never fail. They are new every morning. The same mercy that saves you, keeps you.

Lamentations 3:21-26 – *This I recall to my mind, therefore I have hope. The Lord's lovingkindnesses indeed never cease, for His compassions never fail. They are new every morning; great is Your faithfulness. "The Lord is my portion," says my soul, "therefore I have hope in Him." The Lord is good to those who wait for Him, to the person who seeks Him. It is good that he waits silently for the salvation of the Lord.*

Pray Today

Dear Jesus, Thank you for the gift of mercy. I know the Father's heart is rich in mercy and full of grace, overflowing in love and kindness in my time of need. Thank you for showing me mercy by removing the consequences of my sin and replacing it with the abundant, grace-filled life You promised. Teach me to run to You when I need mercy and help. Let me set aside the pride that keeps me from humbling myself at Your throne. I will wait for You, for You are merciful. Amen.

SANCTIFYING GIFTS
Day 8 – Day 14

For it is God who is at work in you,
both to will and to work for His good pleasure.
Philippians 2:13

Justification and sanctification, gifts of grace,
go together as if tied by an inseparable bond,
so that if anyone tries to separate them,
he is, in a sense, tearing Christ to pieces.
Sanctification doesn't just flow from justification,
so that one produces the other.
Both come from the same Source.
Christ justifies no one whom He does not also sanctify.
By virtue of our union with Christ,
He bestows both gifts, the one never without the other.
–John Calvin[7]

DAY 8: THE GIFT OF TRUTH

> We are either in the process of resisting God's truth
> or in the process of being shaped and molded by his truth.
> - Charles Stanley

John 17:17 – *Sanctify them in the truth; Your word is truth.*

Sanctification begins in truth. In John 17, Jesus prayed for His disciples to be sanctified in the truth and made clear where truth comes from: the Word of God. Jesus sanctifies us with the gift of truth in three specific ways.

Jesus Himself is Truth.

John 14:6 – *Jesus said to him, "I am the way, and the truth, and the life; no one comes to the Father but through Me."*

Truth is not an idea; truth is a Person. When we meet Jesus, we have met truth. When we receive Jesus, we receive truth. Truth is one of God's immutable attributes. God revealed this to Moses when He proclaimed His name to him in Exodus 34:6: *Then the Lord passed by in front of him and proclaimed, "The Lord, the Lord God, compassionate and gracious, slow to anger, and abounding in lovingkindness and truth.* Everything about Jesus is true because Jesus is God. He is the ultimate standard of truth because He is the source of it.

When we are introduced to Jesus, we have one of two reactions. We recognize the truth, and surrender our lives, or we recognize the truth, and run away. The Christian life of sanctification is a continual running to the truth and allowing that truth to penetrate every aspect of our being.

Jesus' Word is Truth.

John 1:1,14 – *In the beginning was the Word, and the Word was with God, and the Word was God. And the Word became flesh, and dwelt among us, and we saw His glory, glory as of the only begotten from the Father, full of grace and truth.*

Psalm 119:160 - *The sum of Your word is truth, and every one of Your righteous ordinances is everlasting.*

We grow in our knowledge of truth through the Word of God, for Jesus is the Word. The written Word instructs us in truth. It is solid, reliable. It is the plumb line for all decisions and all disagreements. In Matthew 7, Jesus warned that the one who hears and acts on His words is wise, and the life built on the Word of God will stand strong in the storms of life. Conversely, the one who hears Jesus' words but refuses to act on or believe them is foolish, and their life will be destroyed. The sanctified life is a result of a deepening knowledge of God's truth in His written Word.

Jesus gives us the Spirit of Truth.

What would life be like if you could never distinguish between truth and falsehood? In today's world of fake news, Photoshop, and video-editing, we can easily be deceived. We must have a personal knowledge of Jesus, a firm conviction in the absolute, irrefutable, inerrant Word of God as the only and final source of truth, but we also need the indwelling Holy Spirit of Truth to guide us and illuminate the Word so we can understand and obey it.

John 14:16-17,26 – *I will ask the Father, and He will give you another Helper, that He may be with you forever; that is the Spirit of truth, whom the world cannot receive, because it does not see Him or know Him, but you know Him because He abides with you and will be in you. But the Helper, the Holy Spirit, whom the Father will send in My name, He will teach you all things, and bring to your remembrance all that I said to you.*

The Holy Spirit enlightens our minds to help us understand truth from God's Word. He gives us discernment to avoid deception. He brings scripture to mind at just the right time. The world is not able to distinguish truth from lies because they do not have the Spirit to guide them; as a Christ-follower, we have the incredible gift of not only knowing the truth but being indwelled by Him.

It is not coincidental that Jesus is called the Light of the World. Light shines in the darkness and exposes the lies that keep us from growing in holiness.

3 John 1:4 – *I have no greater joy than this, to hear of my children walking in the truth.*

Pray Today

Dear Jesus, Thank You for speaking truth to my heart and enlightening my mind to understand it. You are the Truth and Your words are true. What wonderful security and blessing it is to build a life on the foundation of truth. Teach me to walk in truth, in obedience to the Spirit of Truth who guides me through Your Word and gives me discernment in a confusing world where truth is no longer treasured. You are my treasure of truth. Amen.

DAY 9: THE GIFT OF CONVICTION

If there is a sense of panic upon your life,
it may be because there is sin in that life of yours
which you need to get rid of.
- A.W. Tozer[8]

Proverbs 28:13-14 – *He who conceals His transgressions will not prosper, but he who confesses and forsakes them will find compassion. How blessed is the man who fears always, but he who hardens his heart will fall into calamity.*

Have you ever experienced "guilt gut?" When one of our daughters was in the fourth grade, she had a wonderful, but very stern, teacher. She was the kind of teacher that you wanted very much to please, but you were also slightly scared of disappointing or displeasing her. One night, long after bedtime, our daughter came to us crying and upset. She told us that they had taken a test that day in school, and while thinking about her answers, she had been staring off to the side at one of her classmates. When she looked up, her eyes met her teacher's and she immediately perceived that it might appear she had been trying to look at someone else's paper. While that was not the case at all, she *felt* the teacher *might* have thought she was cheating. Her teacher had not confronted her, but that night, she was consumed by what we called "guilt gut." Just the thought of her teacher believing she had cheated caused her conscience to be unsettled. She needed to make things right.

Feeling conviction when we do something wrong is a gift. Conviction starts in our moral conscience, which is the part of our inner man that retains what remains of the image of God in which we were originally created. Sadly, our conscience can become desensitized and even seared so badly by our sinful choices, it no longer serves us well. Our human tendency is to justify or deny our wrongs rather than admit them.

How gracious God is to give us the indwelling, convicting Holy Spirit when we become His children. The Spirit of God is the constant voice in our mind and heart which convicts us of sin, continually molding us into the image of Christ. When God saves us, He immediately begins the work of sanctification, and conviction is a large part of this work. Jesus told his disciples this would happen.

John 16:8-11 – *And He [the Holy Spirit], when He comes, will convict the world concerning sin and righteousness and judgment; concerning sin, because they do not believe in Me; and concerning righteousness, because I go to the Father and you no longer see Me; and concerning judgment, because the ruler of this world has been judged.*

The word *convict* (also translated *reprove*) means to bring to light or expose. It is to call one to account, show him his fault, and demand an explanation. Our flesh rebels against this. No one likes it when his faults or failures are exposed, and we especially don't like to be held accountable for them. But how sad would it be to never know that we were, so to speak, on the wrong side of the law? What if God never convicted us of our sin and we came to the day of judgment unaware? Conviction is God's way of giving us a "heads up" that we're on the wrong path and need to turn around before our sinful choices bring disaster or pain, ending up on the wrong side of *eternity*.

God convicts us because He loves us and desires to remake us into His image. The gift of justification makes us righteous in position; conviction of sin is one gift of sanctification, making us righteous in practice.

When convicted, there are two ways to respond. One is to deny and ignore it, causing our hearts to grow calloused and our spiritual ears to become hard of hearing. This grieves the Spirit of God (Ephesians 4:30). Continued disobedience and rejection of God's loving conviction may reveal that we do not belong to Him after all and need to examine our salvation (2 Corinthians 13:5).

The proper response to conviction is to confess our sins and agree with Him, asking for forgiveness. The very fact that God convicts us reveals His desire for the relationship. It is His "calling card" of pursuit. The gift of conviction may be painful at times to open, but it brings great joy and blessing when it has accomplished its purpose of restoration.

1 John 1:9 - *If we confess our sins, He is faithful and righteous to forgive us our sins and to cleanse us from all unrighteousness.*

Pray Today

Dear Jesus, Thank You for the gift of conviction. When You saved us, You gave us a desire to please You. Our feelings of guilt when we fail to obey You or choose to do things which dishonor You are evidence that Your Spirit does indeed dwell in us. Teach us to respond quickly and confess our sins when we sense the Spirit's conviction in our minds and hearts. Let us run to You in humility and repentance and allow the sweet conviction of Your pursuit to do its work in us. Amen.

DAY 10: THE GIFT OF VICTORY

> Temptations, of course, cannot be avoided, but because we cannot
> prevent the birds from flying over our heads,
> there is no need that we should let them nest in our hair.
> –Martin Luther[9]

1 Corinthians 10:13-14 – *No temptation has overtaken you but such as is common to man; and God is faithful, who will not allow you to be tempted beyond what you are able, but with the temptation will provide the way of escape also, so that you will be able to endure it. Therefore, my beloved, flee from idolatry.*

The gift of victory over temptation is one of the more practical gifts in our pursuit of becoming sanctified Christ-followers, and yet remains one of the most unopened and elusive of all. It is a fact that all believers struggle with sin; it is equally true that, according to scripture, it is a fight we have been equipped to win. In Christ, God promises victory for those who are willing to engage in the battle.

Almost every temptation falls into one of three categories: lust of the flesh (appeals to our body), lust of the eyes (appeals to our soul) and the pride of life (appeals to our spirit). The unredeemed man can only fight against his sinful desires with the strength of a fallen nature; he is spiritually dead and walks in worldliness and corruption (Ephesians 2:1-3). But while the believer's flesh also remains unredeemed, waiting for the physical creation to be renewed (Romans 8:23), his soul has been regenerated and his spirit is indwelled by the powerful, life-giving Spirit of God (Titus 3:5-6). We now have the power to overcome sin.

Jesus removed the penalty and power of sin over our lives, but as we live in a physical world, we are in conflict with the presence of sin. Scripture gives us a simple, practical strategy to follow if we want to enjoy the victory that Christ has given us.

We are to flee from sin.

2 Timothy 2:22 – *Now flee from youthful lusts and pursue righteousness, faith, love and peace, with those who call on the Lord from a pure heart.*

Have you ever found yourself in a situation where you were tempted to sin and recognized the need to simply **run**? Proximity and opportunity are often used by Satan to cause us to fall. Among other things, we are to flee immorality (1 Corinthians 6:18), the love of money (1 Timothy 6:10-11), youthful lusts (2 Timothy 2:22), and idolatry (1 Corinthians 10:14). In the movie, *Fireproof*, a couple is struggling to save their marriage after the husband's addiction to pornography is exposed. He recognizes the powerful draw of having unlimited and private access to his computer, and in righteous anger, he takes it out into the yard and smashes it with a sledgehammer. His neighbors think he has lost his mind, but in a very real way, he is practicing what we all must do when faced with temptation: *flee.*

We are to resist the devil with the Word of God.

James 4:7-8 – *Submit therefore to God. Resist the devil and he will flee from you. Draw near to God and He will draw near to you. Cleanse your hands, you sinners; and purify your hearts, you double-minded.*

In Matthew 4, Jesus modeled how to resist the devil. In every temptation, He responded with truth from God's Word that dismantled Satan's arguments and confirmed His trust in His Father. We are indwelt by the Spirit of God who is far more powerful than the spirit of evil. We dare not attempt to resist the enemy in our own fleshly strength and wisdom, but we are empowered for victory when we respond with the Word. Obviously, the better we know God's Word, the stronger our ability to resist temptation.

We are to draw near to God in watchfulness and prayer.

Matthew 26:41 – *Keep watching and praying that you may not enter into temptation; the spirit is willing, but the flesh is weak.*

On the night He was betrayed, Jesus urged the disciples to watch and pray, knowing what was coming. Giving the final instructions for spiritual warfare, Paul urged the believers at Ephesus to *pray at all times in the Spirit* and to *be on the alert with all perseverance and petition* (Ephesians 6:18). To "watch" is to keep awake and be vigilant; it is to be attentive and ready. We are to live with a heightened sense of alertness of the enemy's attacks and be in an attitude of constant communication with our Father. Whenever temptation comes, we will immediately recognize it and call out to the Father who will give us the way of escape.

Have you unwrapped the gift of victory, or is it languishing unused and unopened? Don't let the enemy steal what God has already given you – power over sin and temptation as a victor in Christ.

Pray Today

Dear Jesus, Thank You for this gift of victory. You came so that I could live victoriously over the sin that separated me from you. Let me live in triumph. Give me wisdom to know when to flee, confidence to apply and obey the Word in every situation, and faithfulness to watch and pray. Amen.

DAY 11: THE GIFT OF FORGIVENESS

We need not climb up into heaven to see whether our sins are forgiven:
let us look into our hearts, and see if we can forgive others.
If we can, we need not doubt but God has forgiven us.
–Thomas Watson[10]

Ephesians 4:32 – *Be kind to one another, tenderhearted, forgiving each other, just as God in Christ also has forgiven you.*

Have you ever "re-gifted" a present you received? Re-gifting occurs when someone gives you something and you pass it on to someone else at a later date. Most likely it's something you never opened or used because you didn't need it. You already had what you needed. As sanctified believers, we need to practice "re-gifting" forgiveness. We need to share from the abundance of what we've been given. Here are three important reasons to nurture the gift of forgiveness.

Forgiveness proclaims our salvation.

Matthew 6:15 – *But if you do not forgive others, then your Father will not forgive your transgressions.*

Jesus spoke about the need for us to forgive others, even making the point if we refuse or are reluctant to forgive, it calls our own salvation into question. In Matthew 6, after teaching the disciples to pray to God to *forgive us our debts, as we also have forgiven our debtors*, He goes on to directly connect God's forgiveness of our sins with our willingness to forgive others. A willingness on our part to show mercy and grace toward others is not a condition of salvation, but rather, evidence that we have been saved. *He who is forgiven little, loves little* (Luke 7:47). Forgiving others shows that we have been forgiven, that we understand what it is to have our sins exposed by a holy God and yet be rescued and restored.

Peter questioned how many times one could be expected to forgive (Matthew 18:21). One Bible scholar proposes that according to the Jewish rabbis, one should expect to forgive the same offense three times. As the prophet Amos indicated God gave the rebellious nations three opportunities to repent, but on the fourth, judgment was dispensed. So according to Jewish tradition, Peter was being magnanimous in suggesting he should forgive seven times.

Instead, Jesus tells us that we ought to forgive seventy times seven, a phrase that essentially meant *unlimited forgiveness*. There is no cap, no maximum. He went on to tell a parable about a servant whose master forgave him a debt he could never pay, but in turn, the servant showed no mercy at all on another man who owed him an exceedingly small amount. When the master found out about it, he called back the forgiven servant, and threw him in prison until the debt could be paid. The point of the story is that we all owe an unpayable debt of sin, yet God forgives all of it. Should we not extend forgiveness to those who have slighted us in ways far less than what we have done in our rebellion against God?

Forgiveness prevents overwhelming sorrow.

2 Corinthians 2:6-7 – *Sufficient for such a one is this punishment which was inflicted by the majority, so that on the contrary you should rather forgive and comfort him, otherwise such a one might be overwhelmed by excessive sorrow.*

Unforgiveness can lead to overwhelming sorrow and emotional and mental defeat in our brothers and sisters. This is why Paul stresses that we ought to be tenderhearted towards others. If a person truly repents and asks forgiveness, let us be quick to restore them to fellowship so that they can continue to grow and mature in their faith. Refusing to forgive others is an act of selfishness on our part, for which we need to seek forgiveness from God ourselves.

Forgiveness provides spiritual protection.

2 Corinthians 2:10-11 – *But one whom you forgive anything, I forgive also; for indeed what I have forgiven, if I have forgiven anything, I did it for your sakes in the presence of Christ, so that no advantage would be taken of us by Satan, for we are not ignorant of his schemes.*

Unforgiveness opens the door to Satan's schemes. Bitterness, hatred, revenge; all of these damaging thoughts and emotions are rooted in unforgiveness. Satan delights to sow discord and conflict so that we are distracted from the purpose and mission God has for us in the gospel. When we forgive, we give testimony to the power of Christ in our lives and leave no room for the enemy's evil strategies to play out.

Is there someone you need to forgive?
Have you been forgiven by God?

Open the gift of forgiveness and move forward in your walk with Christ.

Pray Today

Dear Jesus, Thank You for forgiving me. I owed a debt I could not pay, and You released me from that debt in Your mercy and grace. You paid my sin debt and continue to give me the gift of forgiveness. Teach me how to re-gift again and again the joy of releasing those who have hurt me so that together we can leave sin behind and walk in the new life You came to give us. Amen.

DAY 12: THE GIFT OF THE MIND OF CHRIST

> To "have the mind of Christ" means to look at life from the Savior's point of
> view, having His values and desires in mind.
> It means to think God's thoughts and not think as the world thinks.
> —Warren Wiersbe[11]

1 Corinthians 2:16 – *For who has known the mind of the Lord, that he will instruct Him? But we have the mind of Christ.*

We have the mind of Christ. Taken at face value, we might doubt the truth of that statement. Can we say our minds are always filled with thoughts that please God? What does Paul mean when he makes this bold statement? The answer lies in the context. In 1 Corinthians 2, Paul is teaching us what it means to rely on the indwelling Spirit of God to guide our thoughts, influence our decisions, understand Scripture, and establish a gospel-centered, Christ-honoring worldview.

The Greek word *nous* is translated in two ways: *mind* and *understanding.* It refers to our consciousness which allows us to perceive, understand, and make determinations and judgments. In context of the believer's mind, it indicates our capacity for spiritual truth and the ability to discern between good and evil. We have the *mind of Christ* because God has gifted us with the ability to think and judge from His perspective, because the Spirit of God is in us, thinking God's thoughts.

The natural, unsaved man cannot comprehend spiritual truth; it is foolishness to Him (1 Corinthians 2:14). This is why it is so difficult to convince others to turn to Christ. In fact, we *cannot* convince anyone; they simply cannot understand unless the Spirit of God enlightens their mind. Believers, however, are able to think and reason differently with the mind of Christ. We are able to see truth because Truth dwells *in* us.

Learning to employ the mind of Christ is the key to spiritual maturity; it is our only defense against the deception and false teaching that is so prevalent in our world. This gift must be developed. We must learn to think like Christ, to have God's perspective. Here are three ways we can practically develop the gift of the mind of Christ.

We must determine to set our minds on the Spirit.

Romans 8:5-6 – *For those who are according to the flesh set their minds on the things of the flesh, but those who are according to the Spirit, the things of the Spirit. For the mind set on the flesh is death, but the mind set on the Spirit is life and peace.*

The phrase *set their minds* is the verb *phroneō*, meaning to think or direct one's mind. We must deliberately choose to occupy our minds with spiritual things that honor God and set aside any thoughts that feed our flesh. If you want to break a habit, the best course of action is to replace it with something more desirable. Paul says this another way in Philippians 4:8 when he urges the believers to think about what is true, honorable, right, pure, lovely, etc. As we focus more and more on who God is, we will think less and less about the world.

We must decide to renew our minds daily.

Romans 12:1-2 – *And do not be conformed to this world, but be transformed by the renewing of your mind, so that you may prove what the will of God is, that which is good and acceptable and perfect.*

God's Word is powerful; it is able to change the way we think and feel (Hebrews 4:12). We renew our minds by hearing, reading, studying, meditating, and memorizing scripture. The Bible is the most effective tool available to the Christ-follower for conforming our minds to Christ's. We need "daily downloads" of God's Word that will influence and renew our thinking.

We must deliberately adjust our minds to imitate Christ.

Philippians 2:3-5 – *Do nothing from selfishness or empty conceit, but with humility of mind regard one another as more important than yourselves; do not merely look out for your own personal interests, but also for the interests of others. Have this attitude in yourselves which was also in Christ Jesus.*

A prime example of the mind of Christ is described in Philippians 2:5-11. Christ set aside His own interests and considered our need for salvation. His humility of mind led to complete, sacrificial obedience to the Father. We can deliberately choose to put others first, allowing the Holy Spirit to develop a Christ-like mindset in our daily lives. We can take every thought captive to the obedience of Christ (2 Corinthians 10:5). We can determine to obey God in every part of our lives, mindfully conforming our will to His. This will produce a mind that thinks like Christ, with Christ's interests at heart.

If we have Christ in mind in all things, we will have the mind of Christ.

Pray Today,

Dear Jesus, Thank You for the gift of the mind of Christ. I desire to think as You would think, with Your interests in mind. May my plans and purposes be conformed to Yours as I allow the Holy Spirit to renew my mind through Your Word. Help me to see others as You see them and adjust my thinking to align with Yours. May my every thought be pleasing to You. Amen.

DAY 13: THE GIFT OF WEAKNESS

God specializes in using ordinary people whose limitations and weaknesses
make them ideal showcases for His greatness and glory.
–Nancy Leigh DeMoss[12]

2 Corinthians 12:9-10 – *And He has said to me, "My grace is sufficient for you, for
power is perfected in weakness." Most gladly, therefore, I will rather boast about
my weaknesses, so that the power of Christ may dwell in me. Therefore I am well
content with weaknesses, with insults, with distresses, with persecutions, with
difficulties, for Christ's sake; for when I am weak, then I am strong.*

Like many words, *weakness* is best defined by what it is not. It a lack of
strength. The word is also translated as disease, sickness, and infirmity. You
might think it's odd to include something we avoid at all costs as a "gift" we
receive when we enter into a relationship with Jesus, but in recognizing our
own weaknesses, we find the matchless strength of God.

Light is precious when we are in the dark.
Hope is precious when we are depressed.
Joy is precious when we are grieving.

And so, strength is only precious when we know we are weak.

In Paul's former life, he did not recognize or acknowledge any weakness. He
was a star in his chosen field of Pharisee. His family lineage was perfect. His
power to pursue those he considered enemies was not questioned. I would
imagine he approached his new mission of spreading the gospel with the
same fervency and confidence as his previous passions once God set him on
the path. God gave him great responsibility and revelation in the mysteries
of His eternal purposes and plans. He also gave him a "thorn in the flesh" to
keep him humbly dependent on God's strength, not his own. This was a gift
that was painful in the receiving but produced lasting spiritual fruit as Paul
experienced God's all sufficient, sustaining grace in his weakness.

True faith is man's weakness leaning on God's strength. (D.L. Moody)

God's thinking is always contrary to ours. Aren't we glad? What if we had to earn
our place in God's kingdom? What if responsibility and worth and value were
assigned to us based on how strong we were in our human flesh? What if we had
to pass an I.Q. test, have our skills assessed, and our ancestry examined for any
moral failures before God decided to grant us redemption and forgiveness?

Instead, *God has chosen the foolish things of the world to shame the wise, and God has chosen the weak things of the world to shame the things which are strong ... so that no man may boast before God* (1 Corinthians 1:27,29).

God is not power-hungry; He has no need to prove His strength. *The foolishness of God is wiser than men, and the weakness of God is stronger than men* (1 Corinthians 1:25). To human thinking, the only reason a person would want weak people around him would be to prove his own worth. But God has no need to be affirmed by anyone. God has no weakness, but if we could measure the very least of the smallest exertion of His strength and wisdom possible, it would be beyond our imagination of anything we could hope to attain, even if we could combine all the forces of the strength and wisdom of every human being ever created.

God's exposure of our weakness is for our benefit, not His. He knows that unless we come to the end of ourselves, we will never experience what He desires for us to know – His strength made perfect *in us*.

How does God perfect His strength in us? God's grace sustains us as we allow the Holy Spirit to accomplish His work in and through us. We acknowledge our weakness and ask for His help. The Spirit of God intercedes for us. He stands in our place, empowering us to do what we could never do on our own.

Where are you weak? What are you lacking? In what areas are you feeling helpless and vulnerable? What frailty has God exposed? What limitations do you have? How have you failed?

Acknowledge the weakness, whether it be physical, mental, emotional, or spiritual. Give up trying. Lay down your efforts to serve God in your own strength. Open the gift of weakness and give God the glory.

1 Corinthians 1:30-31 – *But by His doing you are in Christ Jesus, who became to us wisdom from God, and righteousness and sanctification, and redemption, so that, just as it is written, "Let him who boasts, boast in the Lord."*

Pray Today

Dear Jesus, How grateful I am for Your strength made perfect in my weakness. How often have I struggled to do things that You never meant for me to do without You? How gracious it is for You to gently expose our weaknesses, our limitations and our failures in order that we might experience Your unlimited strength and power. Keep us dependent on You. Let us boast in our weaknesses, so that You can get the glory. Amen.

DAY 14: THE GIFT OF HOLINESS

Scripture speaks of both a holiness we already possess in Christ before God
and a holiness in which we are to grow more and more.
The first is the result of the work of Christ for us;
the second is the result of the work of the Holy Spirit in us.
The objective holiness we have in Christ and the subjective holiness
produced by the Holy Spirit are both gifts of God's grace and are
both appropriated by faith.
—Jerry Bridges[13]

1 Peter 1:14-16 – *As obedient children, do not be conformed to the former lusts which were yours in your ignorance, but like the Holy One who called you, be holy yourselves also in all your behavior; because it is written, "You shall be holy, for I am holy."*

If we could find one word that sums up the sanctifying work of God in a believer's life, it would be *holiness*. God is holy, and as He forms us into children who look like their Father, He makes it His business to make us holy. Each gift of sanctification (truth, conviction, victory over temptation, forgiveness, the mind of Christ and weakness) has one goal in mind...our holiness. The object is to strip away all the remains of the old, unregenerate man and reveal the beauty of Christ in us.

As the quote above says, both objective holiness which allows us into heaven, and subjective holiness that gives testimony that we truly belong to God, are gifts of grace. Here are three ways God works to produce holiness in us.

The Spirit makes us holy by His indwelling presence.

1 Corinthians 3:16-17 – *Do you not know that you are a temple of God and that the Spirit of God dwells in you? If any man destroys the temple of God, God will destroy him, for the temple of God is holy, and that is what you are.*

As believers, we are the temple of the Holy Spirit. God has come to dwell in redeemed men and women. Because of His presence in us, we are already counted as holy. God cannot abide in sin. Since the Holy Spirit does indeed live in us, we can be assured that we have been made holy. This is a literal truth, as Paul teaches when he warns against using our physical bodies for immorality. It offends God deeply. We are bought with a price, and our bodies belong to God as a temple for the Holy Spirit (1 Corinthians 7:15-20).

The Father makes us holy through His loving discipline.

Hebrews 12:10 - *For they disciplined us for a short time as seemed best to them, but He disciplines us for our good, so that we may share His holiness.*

God disciplines or chastens us to form His holy character in us. The word means to correct, to instruct, to mold one's character by reproof and admonition. As parents, we discipline our children, not to punish them, but to shape their character. Godly discipline has an outcome in mind; God's goal is that we share His holiness in practical living. The more responsive we are to His correction, the easier this process will be. Conversely, if we are stubborn and resistant to the Father's correction, His hand will be heavy on our lives. The Father's discipline is evidence we belong to the family; He is jealous for His holy name.

The Son makes us holy as His image is formed is us.

Colossians 3:9-10 – *Do not lie to one another, since you laid aside the old self with its evil practices, and have put on the new self who is being renewed to a true knowledge according to the image of the One who created him.*

God chose us in Christ to be holy and blameless before Him before the foundation of the world (Ephesians 1;3-4). We are to be holy in conduct and godliness, anticipating the soon return of the Lord Jesus (2 Peter 3:11). Christ's image is formed in us as we daily lay aside all the sinful desires of our old lives and put on the habits, characteristics, decisions, words, and actions that imitate Christ. One day, the body of Christ, the church, will be presented to Christ as a holy and blameless bride, without spot or wrinkle (Ephesians 5:27, Colossians 1:22).

The Spirit makes us holy in position by His indwelling presence.
The Father makes us holy in practice by His loving discipline.
The Son makes us holy in perfection as His image is formed in us.

How precious is the gift of God's holiness! God is preparing His bride; let this sanctifying gift do its work in you.

2 Corinthians 3:18 – *But we all, with unveiled face, beholding as in a mirror the glory of the Lord, are being transformed into the same image from glory to glory, just as from the Lord, the Spirit.*

Pray Today

Dear Jesus, Thank You for the gift of holiness. You are making me holy, preparing me as Your bride. I long for the day when I am able to look into Your holiness, face to face. Until then, may Your Spirit continue to work in me and may I willingly submit to the Father's discipline until Your image is made perfect in me. Amen.

SATISFYING GIFTS
Day 15 – Day 18

You open Your hand and
satisfy the desire of every living thing.
Psalm 145:16

What are your deepest longings?
Is it to belong, to be accepted, to be truly fulfilled?
We all desire to be affirmed and to know that we matter.
Jesus came to satisfy the desires of our heart with the
abundant life that only He could provide.
He made us family.
He calls us friends.
And by promising an inheritance that will never decay,
He assures us that our souls will be satisfied into eternity.

DAY 15: THE GIFT OF ABUNDANT LIFE

We want to be protected from what can destroy us; we want life.
But we want more than mere life. We want abundant life.
Overflowing life. Deep life. Weighty life. Joyful life.
We don't just want to survive;
we want to thrive at every level of our human being.
We were made for this.
—John Piper[14]

John 10:9-10 – *I am the door; if anyone enters through Me, he will be saved, and will go in and out and find pasture. The thief comes only to steal and kill and destroy; I came that they may have life, and have it abundantly.*

Jesus is the door, the one through whom we gain access to the protection of the sheepfold. He is the Good Shepherd who calls, defends, and lays down His life for His sheep. Salvation is found only in Jesus; no man can come to God or gain heaven in any other way (John 14:6, Acts 4:12). If this were all He offered, it would be enough. Just the *promise* of eternal blessing in the presence of God would sustain us through the few, short years we have to live on this earth.

Thankfully, as we learn to walk with Christ, we realize that Jesus intends for the abundant life to begin now. We gain not only the protection of the sheepfold (our salvation is secure) but we have the privilege of "going in and out to find pasture" (the abundant life of living and walking and enjoying His presence today).

Abundantly is defined as exceeding, over and above, more than is necessary. It is surpassing and extraordinary, super-abundant in quantity and superior in quality. The abundant life found in Christ is the only kind of life that satisfies us; it is the life that God always intended us to have.

Here are four ways God causes us to experience abundant life.

Abundant Grace
Acts 4:33 – *And with great power the apostles were giving testimony to the resurrection of the Lord Jesus, and abundant grace was upon them all.*

In Christ, we are offered abundant grace that exceeds our debt. Paul marveled at this grace when he remembered his former life as a blasphemer and a violent aggressor against those who followed Jesus; he declares *the grace of our Lord was more than abundant* (1 Timothy 1:14). In Romans 5:15-17, he describes this saving grace as abounding to many in far greater measure than the devastating effects of sin. John describes the coming of Jesus as *grace upon grace.* God's grace is abundant – more than enough for us no matter how far we are from God, or how often we come to Him in need of more grace!

Abundant Comfort

2 Corinthians 1:5 – *For just as the sufferings of Christ are ours in abundance, so also our comfort is abundant through Christ.*

In this world, we experience suffering for many reasons. God brings trials to test and refine our faith. We are often tempted. Foolish choices bring unpleasant consequences. Living a godly life and standing on biblical principles brings persecution. Yet God promises comfort that will sustain in direct proportion to the abundance of our suffering. We know Christ by experience; the deeper our pain and suffering, the greater we know His abundant comfort.

Abundant Answers to Prayer

Ephesians 3:20-21 – *Now to Him who is able to do far more abundantly beyond all that we ask or think, according to the power that works within us, to Him be the glory in the church and in Christ Jesus to all generations forever and ever. Amen.*

Think of the greatest answer to your prayers possible, and you will not be able to even imagine what God has in store. We see with limited vision. We can dream up impossible things, but they still fall short of what God can do. His power is unlimited, and His knowledge and insight are infinite. He answers our prayers out of the abundance of His very character and nature, things we cannot yet conceive.

Abundant Reward

2 Peter 1:10-11 – *Therefore, brethren, be all the more diligent to make certain about His calling and choosing you; for as long as you practice these things, you will never stumble; for in this way the entrance into the eternal kingdom of our Lord and Savior Jesus Christ will be abundantly supplied to you.*

Peter writes this promise in context of taking hold of everything God's divine power has granted us through the knowledge of Jesus Christ (2 Peter 1:3). We live abundantly on this earth in faithful obedience, anticipating an abundant "welcome home" from Jesus as He invites us to enter the place He has prepared for us (John 14:1-3), a place beyond our imagination (1 Corinthians 2:9).

Pray Today

Dear Jesus, Thank You for the abundant life that satisfies me in every way. You give me more than I need in every part of life: grace upon grace, all-sustaining comfort, and unimaginable answers to prayer. If that weren't enough, you promised me heaven. I can't wait to hear You say, "Welcome home!" Amen.

DAY 16: THE GIFT OF FAMILY

My kin are those who have been bought by the blood of the Lamb.
They are my brothers and my sisters,
even if they root for the wrong football team.
My calling is to love them like family, for they are family.
They, like me, have been born a second time, born into the family of God.
–R.C. Sproul

Hebrews 2:11 – *For both He who sanctifies and those who are sanctified are all from one Father; for which reason He is not ashamed to call them brethren.*

Does it blow your mind just a little bit that Jesus calls us His brothers and sisters? This idea that we are part of God's family is difficult to fathom. And, perhaps, the word "family" doesn't convey a positive image to you. Our earthly families often let us down and disappoint us. Don't allow your experiences with a temporary, earthly family cause you to miss this precious gift. Jesus came to create a family that lives up to and exceeds all our expectations. He gives us an eternal family.

God defines Himself in relationship to us as our Father throughout scripture. We are born again, a picture of intimacy and love (John 3). We were chosen by God for adoption (Ephesians 1:5-6) and given freedom to call God, *Abba*, a term of endearment, *Daddy* (Romans 8:15). He is truly our *Father*. Jesus said that those of us who do the will of His Father are His brothers and sisters (Matthew 12:50). And what is God's will? To believe in Jesus, to receive the gift of salvation (John 6:40). He promised to return one day and take us to live with Him in our Father's house (John 14:1-3), because that's what families do!

Jesus is our older brother sent by the Father to accomplish what was necessary to secure our place in God's family. The writer of Hebrews tells us *He had to be made like His brethren in all things*, so that He could *bring many sons to glory* (Hebrews 2:10,17). Brethren. Sons. Those are family terms. Put yourself in His place. God created human beings knowing they would need redemption. Jesus was present at creation (let *us* make man in *our* image, Genesis 1:26). He was there when the Father breathed life into Adam and shaped Eve from his rib. He watched as they disobeyed; the woman being deceived but the man deliberately and knowingly choosing his wife over God. Jesus knew that He would have to become like these created beings, setting aside His glory and position in heaven for a time, so that He could taste death on our behalf.

Why would He be willing to do that? Because we're family, and that's what families do for one another. The Father desired us. He wanted to call us His children. There was a job to be done, and the only begotten Son of God was willing to do it. He was willing to rescue those who would become His brothers and sisters. In the most basic sense of the phrase, He put family first.

It's more than enough to contemplate and understand this gift of family as it relates to the Father and the Son. Yet, the blessing of family gained in relationship to Jesus grows that much deeper and wider as we realize we are connected by spiritual DNA to every other true believer, both those still living and those who have gone on to the family homeplace and are waiting for us to arrive. Our immediate family is the church, the body of Christ, and is made up of every person who has put their faith in Jesus looking back on the cross. There's a whole other side of the family, the Old Testament saints, who are also God's children, having come into the family by their faith in the coming Messiah, taking God at His prophetic word and looking forward to the cross. God has been creating His family for an awfully long time and isn't finished yet! In the future, we will welcome brothers and sisters who come out of the Tribulation.

If you belong to Christ, you are part of a huge, rambunctious, diverse family. God's children rarely favor one another; we come in all shapes, sizes, and colors. As siblings do, we often have disagreements and strong opinions. We worship in different ways. Each of us has been created by God with different personalities, quirks, and talents and uniquely gifted at our spiritual birth. Put us all in a room together and you'd find few physical characteristics that reveal our family bond. God delights in our uniqueness as individuals, each of us a masterpiece of His creative workmanship (Ephesians 2:10), yet as we obey the Father, we all grow more and more to look like Jesus, the One whose image is being revealed in us. By the time we get to heaven, our family resemblance to the Father will be clearly seen.

Are you ever lonely? Do you ever feel that you are too different to fit in anywhere? Do you ever feel unloved? Take heart. Jesus brought the gift of family. When you are adopted by faith into God's family, you will never be alone again. You have a Heavenly Father who delights in you, an Elder Brother who gave His life for you, and innumerable siblings all around the world who share your spiritual heritage and family likeness.

Spend some time with the family. It's where you belong.

1 John 3:1a - *See how great a love the Father has bestowed on us, that we would be called children of God; and such we are.*

Pray Today

Dear Jesus, Thank You for making me part of Your family. How precious to know that we belong. You have blessed us with many, many siblings so that we will never feel alone. We look forward to the day when we will all gather around the Father's table and share how good it is to be part of the family. Amen.

DAY 17: THE GIFT OF FRIENDSHIP

Mutual communion is the soul of all true friendship,
and a familiar converse with a friend hath the greatest sweetness in it...
[so] besides the common tribute of daily worship you owe to [God],
take occasion to come into His presence on purpose
to have communion with Him.
—J.I. Packer[15]

John 15:13-15 – *Greater love has no one than this, that one lay down his life for his friends. You are My friends if you do what I command you. No longer do I call you slaves, for the slave does not know what his master is doing; but I have called you friends, for all things that I have heard from My Father I have made known to you.*

Jesus defines real friendship. The word for friend is *philos* and means "loved" or "dear." The root word is *phileo* and describes an affectionate love built on shared interests.

In John 15:12-17, Jesus begins and ends with the same admonition to His disciples: *love one another.* In between, He tells us what loving one another looks like by His own example of friendship.

Real friendship calls for complete sacrifice.

Jesus set the bar high. *No greater love.* Jesus is our friend because *He lay down His life* for us. Do you have a friend that you would be willing to die for? Is there someone who loves you enough to die for you? *Yes.* Jesus.

Jesus demonstrated the highest level of friendship, that of complete sacrifice. He gave up Himself. He set aside His own glory and became obedient to death (Philippians 2), displaying the highest level of love for those He called friends.

Real friendship calls for complete honesty.

Have you ever had a friend lie to you? Dishonesty will end a friendship faster than anything. Jesus is a true friend; He assures us that He has communicated the Father's plans and purposes. He has no hidden agenda. He has told us what the Father wants us to know.

What is Jesus' message? Truth about our sin. Truth about our need for salvation. Truth about repentance. And truth about who He is, the Son of God, who loves us so much He died for us.

God gave us the gift of friendship in Jesus. How can we return this friendship? Can we be a friend of God, as He is our friend? Jesus says we are His friends if we do what He commands us.

Jesus commands us to lay down our lives, just as He did.

Matthew 16:24 – *Then Jesus said to His disciples, "If anyone wishes to come after Me, he must deny himself, and take up his cross and follow Me.*

Abraham was called the friend of God because He believed and obeyed when God asked him to sacrifice his son, Isaac (James 2:23). He had learned the secret of friendship with God; he set aside his own interests and instead pursued God's interests. He was willing to give up the most precious thing in the world to him, in obedience to God's command, trusting that God was able to raise Isaac from the dead. He showed that he was a true friend of God.

Jesus commands us to love one another.

John 15:17 – *This I command you, that you love one another.*

Loving others is an overflow of our love for God. *We love, because He first loved us* (1 John 4:19). A good example of this is Moses, who had such a special relationship with God that He spoke to him "face to face, just as a man speaks to his friend" (Exodus 33:11). Moses often lingered in the Tent of Meeting, communing with God, enjoying His presence. This carried over into Moses' love for His people – that stubborn, ungrateful group that complained and argued and disobeyed while Moses led them out of slavery. He sought God's mercy many times for them, even offering to be blotted out of God's book on their behalf, if it meant God would forgive them! (Exodus 32:32)

Jesus loves us deeply, affectionately. He laid down His life for us, and He tells us the truth. When we meet Jesus, we meet our truest friend who shows us by example how to be a friend to others. Spend time with Jesus and discover the gift of real friendship.

Proverbs 17:17a – *A friend loves at all times.*

Pray Today

Dear Jesus, Thank You for being my true friend. You sacrificed Yourself for me, and You are always honest with me. Your gift of friendship allows me to love others and be the kind of friend to them, that You are to me. Teach me to set aside my interests on behalf of others, and in obedience to You. Amen.

DAY 18: THE GIFT OF INHERITANCE

It is God's great plan that every believer one day "become conformed to the image of His Son." That is the hope of His calling – the eternal destiny and glory of the believer fulfilled in the coming kingdom. The fullness of that hope will be experienced when we receive the supreme riches of the glory of His inheritance in the saints. ...
Our being glorious children of God and joint heirs with Jesus Christ of all God possesses is the consummation and end of salvation promised from eternity past and held in hope until the future manifestation of Christ.
–John MacArthur[16]

1 Peter 1:3-4 – *Blessed be the God and Father of our Lord Jesus Christ, who according to His great mercy has caused us to be born again to a living hope through the resurrection of Jesus Christ from the dead, to obtain an inheritance which is imperishable and undefiled and will not fade away, reserved in heaven for you.*

By its very nature, an inheritance is a gift. It is held in trust until all the terms of the will are met, most likely a death. An inheritance often has stipulations which must be met before an heir can take possession. This is true of our inheritance in Christ as well; it is only for those who are born again by the will of God.

Ephesians 1:11-12 – *In Him also we have obtained an inheritance, having been predestined according to His purpose who works all things after the counsel of His will, to the end that we who were the first to hope in Christ would be to the praise of His glory.*

God planned our inheritance long ago when He chose us before the foundation of the world (Ephesians 1:4). He pursued us; we simply responded to the work of God's Spirit enlightening us to understand the gospel. We do not earn our inheritance but receive it as a gift of grace. It is only accessible in Christ.

Our inheritance can be defined as the fulfillment of all the promises of God that result in our transformation into perfect Christlikeness (Romans 8:29), with access to all that God has. We will be translated into immortality to live forever in the presence of Jesus (1 Thessalonians 4:17, 1 Corinthians 15:52-53). It is the completion of our redemption when we lay aside this fallen, human flesh (our temporary earthly house) and are clothed with the dwelling not made by human hands, our eternal home (2 Corinthians 5:2-5).

One of the blessings of being in Christ is that we do not have to wait until heaven to benefit from our inheritance. God gives us a pledge, or down payment as a promise or guarantee of what is to come. We can access the benefits of our inheritance even now!

Ephesians 1:13-14 – *In Him, you also, after listening to the message of truth, the gospel of your salvation – having also believed, you were sealed in Him with the Holy Spirit of promise, who is given as a pledge of our inheritance, with a view to the redemption of God's own possession, to the praise of His glory.*

The Spirit's work is to sanctify us and His work in us is intimately tied to our inheritance. Paul reminds us that the inheritance belongs to those who are sanctified (Acts 20:32, 26:18). Just as a mortal being cannot inherit heaven, neither can those who refuse to be sanctified (Galatians 5:21, Ephesians 5:5).

If you've experienced the sanctifying conviction of the Holy Spirit, you know it can be a painful process; we don't normally connect this to the joyful idea of receiving a heavenly inheritance. But here's the truth we can delight in. If our inheritance consists of finally being made whole and perfect and righteous, then every time the Spirit convicts us or shows us things in our lives that must be addressed, we can rejoice because it confirms the promise that we truly belong to God and are in line to inherit! His work in us is a *guarantee* or *pledge* we will receive in full what God holds in trust. We will be made perfect.

God doesn't want our inheritance to be a mystery. Paul prays for the believers in Ephesus to know what's in store, so that they can faithfully experience the reality of the coming hope, even in the present days of difficulty and trials (Ephesians 1:18-19a). The more we experience the overcoming power of the Holy Spirit in us today, the more clearly we see what awaits us in heaven tomorrow.

The good news is that God never gives up on us and rewrites His will! Our inheritance is secure, because it is not dependent on us, but given *in Christ.* It is reserved in heaven for us; it is imperishable, undefiled and will not fade away. God will have His immortal children. He will get us home just as He promised.

Ephesians 1:18-19a – *I pray that the eyes of your heart may be enlightened, so that you will know what is the hope of His calling, what are the riches of the glory of His inheritance in the saints, and what is the surpassing greatness of His power toward us who believe.*

Pray Today

Dear Jesus, Thank You for sharing Your inheritance with me! Your Word tells me that I am a "joint-heir" with You. All of God's promises are mine in You. Help me to live with anticipation. Give me wisdom and humility to surrender to the sanctifying work of Your Holy Spirit as He prepares me to inherit the kingdom. Amen.

SERVING GIFTS
Day 19 – Day 24

Whatever you do, do your work heartily,
as for the Lord rather than for men,
knowing that from the Lord
you will receive the reward of the inheritance.
It is the Lord Christ whom you serve.
Colossians 3:23-24

Jesus came to give purpose and meaning to our lives.
He commissions us as His ambassadors.
We are citizens of another kingdom on assignment for the Master.
In His wisdom and sovereignty, He gifts us with exactly the
talents, abilities, and skills required to carry out the mission.
We are servants of the Savior; we have all the gifts we need.

DAY 19: THE GIFT OF SPIRITUAL GIFTS

Each of us has one spiritual gift, a blend of the different gifts
the Spirit has put together for each of us.
Like a painter who is able to create an infinite number of colors by mixing
any combination of the ten or so colors he carries in his palette,
so the Spirit of God blends a little of one gift
with a little of another to create the perfect combination within you.
As a result, you have a unique position in the Body of Christ,
with an ability to minister as no one else can.
–John MacArthur[17]

1 Corinthians 12:4-6,11 – *Now there are varieties of gifts but the same Spirit. And there are varieties of ministries, and the same Lord. There are varieties of effects, but the same God who works all things in all persons. But one and the same Spirit works all these things, distributing to each one individually just as He wills.*

As a student of scripture, I like my lists. I love it when God makes something so clear there can be no doubt or discussion on its meaning. I like to organize my theology and understanding of God into neat boxes I can check off. Fortunately, I serve a God who is not limited to my charts and graphs! He is far more creative, and this is stunningly visible in the way He gifts His children.

Every person who comes to faith in Christ is given one or more spiritual gifts which are to be used for the growth of God's kingdom and the maturing of the body. Some of these gifts are listed in scripture (1 Corinthians 12, Romans 8) and there are a multitude of tests and surveys that can help a believer discover their gifts. Even so, we should not label ourselves to the extent we limit what God is able to develop in us and accomplish through us when we are completely submitted to the Holy Spirit.

The verses above are a beautiful explanation of how God allows us to experience Him as we serve Him, offering the gifts of grace He has bestowed on us back to Him. The word *varieties* (also translated *diversities*) has a literal meaning of "to take apart." If the body of Christ (all true believers) were personified as a large painting, and we could focus in and separate each individual brush stroke that contributed to the final image, we would have "taken apart" the painting. We would see the diversity and variety of colors, brush techniques, and paint materials that were necessary to produce a masterpiece.

Listen to Paul's words in Ephesians 2:10: *For we are His workmanship [i.e. masterpiece], created in Christ Jesus for good works, which God prepared beforehand so that we would walk in them.* Later on, in Ephesians 4:12-13, in context of teaching about the purpose of spiritual gifts, he says, *for the equipping of the saints for the work of service, to the building up of the body of Christ; until we all attain to the unity of the faith, and of the knowledge of the Son of God, to a mature man, to the measure of the stature which belongs to the fullness of Christ.*

God never distributes spiritual gifts with the individual in mind. His goal is a complete body, all members working together to complete the image of Christ to the world. Our gifts are meant to produce one masterpiece, the complete body of Christ.

To accomplish this, spiritual gifts are distributed with the full participation of the Trinity – God the Father, Jesus the Son, and the Holy Spirit.

Gifts come from the Holy Spirit.
Ministries come from the Lord, Jesus.
Effects come from God, the Father.

When a person is born again, the Spirit of God gifts them with one or more spiritual **gifts**. As we learn to *walk in the same manner as Jesus* (1 John 2:6), imitating Christ and being conformed to His image, we will employ our gifts in various types of **ministries**. Literally, we are the hands and feet of Jesus. As these ministries expand and impact our families, neighborhoods, cities, and our world, they will have an **effect** which has been designed and orchestrated by God the Father, who is sovereign over all. We accomplish His work in this world, because we have used our giftedness in ministries to proclaim Christ.

In Jesus, we are uniquely, intentionally, and divinely gifted. He came to make more of your life than you can imagine. Open the gifts He's given you and put them to use in the kingdom. Every single brush stroke is precious to the Master who designed us.

1 Peter 4:10 – *As each one has received a special gift, employ it in serving one another as good stewards of the manifold grace of God.*

Pray Today

Dear Jesus, You have given us so many gifts that we treasure, but the gifts of grace given by the Holy Spirit are one that we can give back to You. We see Your creativity in the faces and abilities of our brothers and sisters in this unique family we call the body of Christ. Teach us to use our gifts to serve one another so that the world will take notice of the beauty and glory of the Savior, whom we serve. Help us to work together to develop, strengthen and utilize the gifts of every person, for we are all equally important and necessary to finish the masterpiece of the image of Christ. Amen.

Day 20: The Gift Of Purpose

The most glorious reason you exist is for the
proclamation of the glory of God to the ends of the world.
And it's more than having a nice life.
—David Platt[18]

Romans 15:4-6 – *For whatever was written in earlier times was written for our instruction, so that through perseverance and the encouragement of the Scriptures we might have hope. Now may the God who gives perseverance and encouragement grant you to be of the same mind with one another according to Christ Jesus, so that with one accord you may with one voice glorify the God and Father of our Lord Jesus Christ.*

One of the most distinguishing characteristics of a follower of Christ is their motivation and purpose for life. Before we meet Jesus, we live for ourselves. We may spend a lot of time doing good things for other people. We may see ourselves as blessed and give generously to causes we believe in. But ultimately, without Christ at the center, we live primarily to benefit ourselves.

Jesus offers us the gift of purpose, of discovering the reason we were created and continue to exist. *We were made to worship God.*

To those who have yet to meet Jesus, the idea of a God who desires the worship of His creation sounds rather self-serving. Who is God to demand our allegiance and loyalty? Declaring oneself as worthy of worship seems presumptuous and egocentric. No one likes a narcissist. It is only when we have met Christ that we begin to understand that worshipping God is not a burden or a duty. Instead, worship is coming home. It is finding the place that we were always intended to live. It is realizing and experiencing the only thing that will ever satisfy and fulfill us as created beings made to worship the Creator.

When our life's purpose is to worship and glorify God, everything makes perfect sense. We have a greater, higher reason for every decision, every action, every word. How we spend our money, how we use our time, where we go and what we do when we're there...all of it has value and meaning when it's centered on what brings glory to God.

How can we enjoy the gift of purpose and glorify God with our lives?

We worship God by honoring Him in our daily activities.

1 Corinthians 10:31 - *Whether, then, you eat or drink or whatever you do, do all to the glory of God.*

Worship doesn't just happen on Sunday. Worship takes place when we consider God in the everyday, ordinary, and mundane. Scripture gives us God's instructions for eating, drinking, working, playing, socializing, raising children, caring for parents, being a good neighbor, and the thousand other things that fill up our days. A worshipper asks the question, "How can I honor God in this?" in the little things we think are irrelevant to God, as well as the big things.

We worship God by growing into Christlikeness.

2 Corinthians 3:18 – *But we all, with unveiled face, beholding as in a mirror the glory of the Lord, are being transformed into the same image from glory to glory, just as from the Lord, the Spirit.*

Nothing honors God more than our desire to be like Him. When we obey His commands, surrender to His conviction, and do the hard work of saying "no" to the flesh and "yes" to the Spirit, we are worshipping God. Striving to be like Jesus honors the Father in a very tangible, practical way.

We worship God by telling others about Him.

Philippians 2:10-11 – *So that at the name of Jesus EVERY KNEE WILL BOW, of those who are in heaven and on earth and under the earth, and that every tongue will confess that Jesus Christ is Lord, to the glory of God the Father.*

All people will one day bow their knees and worship God. How could we honor Him more than by making it our life's mission to proclaim the gospel of Jesus, so that others have the opportunity to worship God as Savior, and not as the Righteous Judge who will condemn them for their sin? We will worship God for eternity; let's honor the gift of a life of purpose by sharing that good news with others.

Pray Today

Dear Jesus, Thank You for filling my life with purpose and meaning. You have given us a mission, to tell others about You. We do this by purposely centering our lives around You, honoring You in everything we do, and speaking about You. We want You to be clearly seen; help us to worship You in every part of our lives. Amen.

DAY 21: THE GIFT OF KINGDOM

I place no value on anything I have or may possess,
except in relation to the kingdom of God.
If anything will advance the interests of the kingdom,
it shall be given away or kept, only as by giving or keeping it
I shall most promote the glory of Him
to whom I owe all my hopes in time or eternity.
—David Livingston

Colossians 1:13 – *For He rescued us from the domain of darkness, and transferred us to the kingdom of His beloved Son.*

Those of us who live under democratic governments do not think much about kings and kingdoms. In America, the last king we served was the King George III; our freedom was won at the cost of war, and many patriots gave their lives to establish a new kind of nation governed by elected officials tasked to serve the people, not the other way around.

Perhaps that's one reason we struggle to recognize the beauty of Jesus as King. We see kings as tyrants; experience has taught us that too much power over our lives in the hands of a governing authority is never a good thing.

But Jesus is a different kind of king! He is not king because we selected Him or crowned Him; He is King because He is God. He is the very definition of a good king, being completely righteous and unable to do wrong. He always acts in the best interest of His subjects. He is all powerful, all-knowing, and omnipresent. He knows everything about us. There is no higher authority; He is King of kings and Lord of lords.

When Jesus appeared on the scene, John the Baptist preached, "*Repent, for the kingdom of heaven is at hand*" (Matthew 3:2). Jesus came to bring the kingdom of God to us, and invite us in. He came to rescue us from Satan's domain, which He accomplished through His death. He nailed the accusations of our sin to the cross; Satan no longer has any power or hold on us. We are free to enter God's kingdom and worship Jesus as the only true King.

If only we could see ourselves as citizens of the Kingdom! Here are three reasons to delight in Jesus as our King and enjoy the gift of His kingdom.

#1 – Kingdom citizenship is gained by grace.

Luke 12:32 – *Do not be afraid, little flock, for your Father has chosen gladly to give you the kingdom.*

We don't earn our place in the kingdom; we are invited in as guests of the King. He opens our eyes to see the truth (2 Corinthians 4:6). He grants us repentance (2 Timothy 2:25). He provides faith to believe (Ephesians 2:8). We become citizens of the kingdom by the kindness and grace of Jesus, the King.

#2 – Kingdom citizenship provides for our needs.

Matthew 6:33 – *But seek first His kingdom and His righteousness, and all these things will be added to you.*

Being part of Jesus' kingdom means we never have to worry. In Matthew 6:25-34, Jesus taught us to set aside all anxiety about food, clothing, shelter, even our very lives because the Father knows exactly what we need and will provide. He has the resources of the universe at His disposal and is able to create what is not yet created should that be necessary. As we seek the King, we have a better different understanding of what we really need. We can trust Jesus to take care of His kingdom.

#3 – Kingdom citizenship extends beyond this world.

John 18:36 – *Jesus answered, "My kingdom is not of this world. If My kingdom were of this world, then My servants would be fighting so that I would not be handed over to the Jews; but as it is, My kingdom is not of this realm."*

There is a heavenly kingdom yet to be explored. Jesus' kingdom is a spiritual kingdom which we enjoy now with all the rights and privileges of citizenship. Yet to come is Jesus' physical kingdom which will be set up on earth, and after that, an eternal kingdom whose reality and dimension we cannot even imagine. Kingdom citizenship offers an eternal life in the presence of the King.

Are you tired of living under the rules and regulations of this world? Take heart, you have been given the gift of the kingdom. You are serving the real King and will one day worship at His throne, welcomed as a citizen of the kingdom of God.

2 Timothy 4:18 – *The Lord will rescue me from every evil deed, and will bring me safely to His heavenly kingdom; to Him be the glory forever and ever. Amen.*

Pray Today

Dear Jesus, How precious it is to know that we are citizens of the kingdom of God! You reign over all the world, and we are privileged to be Your children, Your servants, and Your citizens. We can't wait to explore the heavenly kingdom, but even more, to come into Your throne room and worship You face to face. Keep our hearts and minds focused on Your kingdom, the kingdom of God. Amen.

DAY 22: THE GIFT OF FRUIT

> As the apple is not the cause of the apple tree, but a fruit of it:
> even so good works are not the cause of our salvation,
> but a sign and a fruit of the same.
> –Daniel Cawdray[19]

John 15:4-5,8 – *Abide in Me, and I in you. As the branch cannot bear fruit of itself unless it abides in the vine, so neither can you unless you abide in Me. I am the vine, you are the branches; he who abides in Me and I in him, he bears much fruit, for apart from Me you can do nothing. My Father is glorified by this, that you bear much fruit, and so prove to be My disciples.*

When God created Adam and Eve, He had something in mind for them to do. As New Testament Christ-followers, we are familiar with Jesus' teaching that we ought to bear fruit. But are you aware that the very first words recorded that God spoke to Adam and Eve were **be fruitful**?

God was speaking in a literal sense. He wanted Adam and Eve to bear children and populate the earth. But the point is clear. God is all about life. What He created, He designed to reproduce. It's easy to see in the physical world, and it's just as important in the spiritual. God desires for our spiritual life to reproduce, to *bear fruit.*

The good news is that He divinely equips us to bear fruit. We cannot produce spiritual fruit with physical, fleshly efforts. Bearing fruit is an overflow of our connection to the Father. Jesus' explanation of the vine and the branches is a beautiful picture of the gift of fruit that is ours in Him, and in Him alone. Fruit proves that we belong to Him; it is a result, not a cause of salvation.

Remember the story of the "ugly duckling?" He couldn't figure out why he looked so different from the ducks. He wanted to fit in, but they rejected him. They instinctively knew he didn't belong. His DNA exposed him. As he matured, it became clear that he wasn't a duck at all; he was a beautiful white swan. In the same way, as we grow up in Christ, our spiritual DNA reveals who we are in Christ. We bear fruit.

Here are three ways the gift of fruit is made effective in our lives.

#1 – Christ-followers bear the fruit of good character.
Galatians 5:22-23 – *But the fruit of the Spirit is love, joy, peace, patience, kindness, goodness, faithfulness, gentleness, self-control; against such things there is no law.*

How hard is it for you to manufacture peace in your own heart? Try as you might, you just can't do it. Peace is a gift, a fruit of the indwelling Spirit of God. Notice "fruit" is singular; these are not "fruits" we produce from our own efforts, but results that come when we are surrendered and submitted to God's Spirit. They are rooted in our relationship with God. We love others because our hearts are filled with the love of God. We have the peace *of* God because we have peace *with* God. We have patience because God is patient with us. And so on. The closer we lean into Christ, the greater the fruit of the Spirit will be born out in us.

#2 – Christ-followers bear the fruit of good works.
Colossians 1:10 – *So that you will walk in a manner worthy of the Lord, to please Him in all respects, bearing fruit in every good work and increasing in the knowledge of God.*

God planned good works for us long before He saved us (Ephesians 2:10). He has things for us to accomplish for the kingdom, but they are not of our own doing. *It is God who is at work in you, both to will and to work for His good pleasure* (Philippians 2:13). In other words, God gifts us with both the desire and the ability to accomplish the fruit of good works. As we abide in Him, He directs our steps, prompts our thoughts, inspires our words, and accomplishes His work through us. We bear the fruit of good works.

#3 – Christ-followers bear the fruit of good news.
Proverbs 11:30 – *The fruit of the righteous is a tree of life, And he who is wise wins souls.*

God told Adam and Eve to *be fruitful and multiply*, meaning physical children. While we still obey this command as He blesses us with babies, we are also called to bear spiritual children by sharing the good news of the gospel. Jesus illustrated this principle in the parable of the sower: when the Word of God fell on good soil, it reproduced thirty, sixty, a hundredfold! Paul often talked of the gospel bearing fruit, and prayed for it to spread, meaning be reproduced as Jesus' followers continued to speak. We don't produce fruit; we simply plant the seeds of the gospel and watch them bear fruit.

Fruit is a gift produced by the Holy Spirit because we have been given spiritual life in Jesus. It's His character, His works, and His gospel. Are you bearing fruit? Rejoice ... your spiritual DNA is showing!

Pray Today

Dear Jesus, Thank You for giving us the privilege of being "fruit-bearers." We cannot produce any spiritual life by our own efforts, but when we are surrendered and obedient to the Holy Spirit, our lives will overflow with fruit that honors You. Teach us to be willing participants as You reproduce Your character in us, and invite us into Your work in this world, and the spread of Your gospel. Amen.

DAY 23: THE GIFT OF HELP

The more we see our frailty, weakness, and dependence, the more we
appreciate God's grace in its dimension of His divine assistance.
Just as grace shines more brilliantly against the dark background of our sin, so
it also shines more brilliantly against the background of our human weakness.
–Jerry Bridges[20]

Hebrews 4:16 – *Therefore let us draw near with confidence to the throne of grace,
so that we may receive mercy and find grace to help in time of need.*

In his book, *The Normal Christian Life*, Watchman Nee shares that he and several
other brothers in Christ were swimming in a river one day, when he noticed that
a man began to sink when his leg cramped. Nee motioned to the best swimmer
in their group to save his friend, but to his dismay, the expert swimmer delayed,
making no move towards the drowning man. The group grew very agitated, not
able to understand why this man would let a friend drown. Finally, when the
man gave up striving to stay afloat and truly began to sink, the swimmer was at
his side in a few short strokes and brought him safely to shore. The lesson? The
expert swimmer knew that until the man gave up trying, he would fight his
rescuer and take them both under. He knew to wait until the drowning man
recognized his need of help; then and only then could his friend carry him to
safety.[21]

The moral of the story is about the rescued, not the rescuer. God is certainly not
too weak to save us when we are fighting against Him. He could override our
resistance at any time, but in His sovereignty, He waits for us to recognize our
need. Jesus has brought to us the gift of help, but until we are humble enough to
ask for it, God will allow us to struggle. Speaking to the Israelites in Isaiah 30:15-
18, God says it is *in repentance and rest* we will be saved, that our strength is
found in *quietness and trust*. Unfortunately, the children of Israel were not
willing to trust God and ask Him for help. They tried to defend themselves, to use
their own resources and human alliances for protection. In response, God said
He longed to be gracious, and *He waits on high to have compassion.*

He waits. He is waiting for us to give up and ask for help.

Help from God is not some vague spiritual idea whereby we simply adjust our
thinking and trust that things will turn out well for us in the end. Yes, we do
change our thoughts to be in line with His eternal perspective, and yes, we know
the end of the story; it *will* turn out for our good (Romans 8:28). But God's help
is also tangible, practical. He acts deliberately on behalf of His children. He
intervenes in the circumstances of our world. He is not distant, ruling from afar,

watching us struggle in vain. He is *with us* in our hardships. When we humble ourselves to ask, help is there, a gift we have access to because of Jesus.

In Genesis 2:18, God said it was not good for man to be alone, so He provided a *helper* for Adam; He created Eve. In 1 Chronicles 12:22, after David was made king, *day by day men came to David to help him, until there was a great army like the army of God*. David knew God's hand was in this, just as Nehemiah recognized when the people gathered together with a mind to work and rebuilt the walls around Jerusalem in the record time of fifty-two days. Those who opposed the work lost their confidence, recognizing *this work had been accomplished with the help of God* (Nehemiah 6:15-16).

The psalms are full of prayers and praises for the help God provides to the hurting, the sick, the persecuted, and the one who is overwhelmed with life.

Psalm 33:20 – *Our soul waits for the Lord; He is our help and our shield.*
Psalm 46:1 – *God is our refuge and strength, a very present help in trouble.*
Psalm 121:1-2 – *I will lift up my eyes to the mountains; from where shall my help come? My help comes from the Lord, Who made heaven and earth.*

Jesus brings this gift of help to us even more personally with the promise of the Holy Spirit, who He described as another *Helper*. The word is *paraklētos*, also translated *Comforter*. The literal meaning is "called to one's side" as an advocate, able to give aid. Knowing the disciples were full of sorrow because He was leaving them, Jesus promised they would be well-taken care of, as He would ask the Father to send the Spirit. We have divine help available at all times, in all places, and in all situations.

What if you are ready and willing to receive the help offered in Jesus, but aren't even sure what to ask? No worries: the Holy Spirit is there too, interceding for us, communicating our deepest heart-needs to the Father, and ministering to us.

Do you have need? Stop struggling. Give it up and open the gift of help.

Romans 8:26-27 – *In the same way the Spirit also helps our weakness; for we do not know how to pray as we should, but the Spirit Himself intercedes for us with groanings too deep for words; and He who searches the hearts knows what the mind of the Spirit is, because He intercedes for the saints according to the will of God.*

Pray Today

Dear Jesus, Thank You for the gift of help. There is no need too great for You to handle. We are never too lost, too discouraged or in too much trouble. We only need to come to You, the only One who offers real help. Teach us to humble ourselves, stop struggling and take hold of You. Amen.

DAY 24: THE GIFT OF WISDOM

To search for wisdom apart from Christ means not simply foolhardiness
but utter insanity.
–John Calvin

James 1:5 – *But if any of you lacks wisdom, let him ask of God, who gives to all generously and without reproach, and it will be given to him.*

Wisdom is more than the accumulation of knowledge; it is the ability to put that knowledge to good use. Wisdom is akin to discernment, perception. In some cases, it's simple common sense. It is the ability to perceive more than what is seen on the surface in any given circumstance and have the judgment to determine the best course of action.

Godly wisdom involves having God's viewpoint; it is seeing life from His perspective, in light of His commands, and making the necessary adjustments. A wise person is able (and willing) to apply God's Word to his life in practical, tangible ways, to achieve the purposes and plans revealed by God therein.

Human wisdom is limited both in scope and usefulness. Human knowledge is incomplete. Our understanding is skewed by self-focus, and our fleshly minds are fallen and depraved. Despite what the philosophy teachers tell you, we cannot think our way to a higher plane. Real wisdom, life-changing, eternal wisdom comes only from God, and is a gift. *For the Lord gives wisdom; from His mouth come knowledge and understanding* (Proverbs 2:6).

The gift of godly wisdom begins with the proper view of God.
Proverbs 9:10 – *The fear of the Lord is the beginning of wisdom, And the knowledge of the Holy One is understanding.*

Wisdom must be rooted in a correct recognition of God's authority and character. He is our Creator, and we answer to Him. He is holy, righteous, and just. He is always and only good. He will never lie to us, deceive us, or betray us. He loves mercy. He is full of grace and compassion. He is to be feared as the one true God, the Most Holy ruler of all that exists.

The gift of godly wisdom is more valuable than any material possession.
Proverbs 16:16 – *How much better it is to get wisdom than gold! And to get understanding is to be chosen above silver.*

Happy homes are not built on bank accounts. A person may have access to everything they could possibly want or need and still be empty, disillusioned, and lost. Do you want a purpose-filled, productive, joyful life? Pursue the godly wisdom, understanding and knowledge that will fill your life with precious and pleasant riches (Proverbs 24:3-4).

The gift of godly wisdom must be mined from the treasure of God's Word.
2 Timothy 3:14-17 – *You, however, continue in the things you have learned and become convinced of, knowing from whom you have learned them, and that from childhood you have known the sacred writings which are able to give you the wisdom that leads to salvation through faith which is in Christ Jesus. All scripture is inspired by God and profitable for teaching, for reproof, for correction, for training in righteousness; so that the man of God may be adequate, equipped for every good work.*

Paul had every confidence that Timothy would be a wise and effective pastor; his life was built on the scriptures. Wisdom is not mysterious or elusive. God has given us a literal treasure trove in His written Word. When we open God's Word and ask the Holy Spirit to illuminate and enlighten our minds to understand it, we have access to the very thoughts and knowledge of God. There is no greater wisdom than the Word of God, and no other place to find it.

The gift of godly wisdom stands in stark contrast to man's wisdom.
1 Corinthians 3:18-20 – *Let no man deceive himself. If any man among you thinks that he is wise in this age, he must become foolish, so that he may become wise. For the wisdom of this world is foolishness before God. For it is written, "He is the one who catches the wise in their craftiness;" and again, "The Lord knows the reasonings of the wise, that they are useless."*

If you want to live a life governed by the wisdom of God, expect to stand out. God's wisdom is foolishness to the world and will most likely guide you in the opposite direction of where everyone else is headed. If what God's Word is telling you is something that your unbelieving friends think is unwise, weird, or just plain senseless, it's a good sign you're on the path of godly wisdom!

Don't spend another day in foolish, worldly thinking. Open the gift of wisdom Jesus came to give you. It's the sensible thing to do.

Psalm 90:12 – *So teach us to number our days, That we may present to You a heart of wisdom.*

Pray Today

Dear Jesus, You are wisdom personified, and You came in human flesh to show us the ways of God's wisdom. How foolish we are to stumble along in life in our limited understanding, when You desire to show us a far, far better way. Your wisdom is practical and relevant to our daily lives. Teach us to ask for Your wisdom and give us willing hearts to listen and obey the insight You promise to provide. Amen.

STRENGTHENING GIFTS
Day 25 – Day 29

Do not fear, for I am with you; Do not anxiously look about you,
for I am your God. I will strengthen you, surely I will help you,
surely I will uphold you with My righteous right hand.
Isaiah 41:10

Jesus came to give us the strength to serve the kingdom.
When He had completed His mission on earth,
He returned to heaven and sent us the gift of the Holy Spirit
who protects us, secures us, gives us courage,
helps us when we don't know how to pray,
and leads us through the trials that strengthen our faith.

DAY 25: THE GIFT OF THE HOLY SPIRIT

When it is a question of God's Almighty Spirit,
never say, "I can't."
–Oswald Chambers

Ephesians 3:14-21 – *For this reason I bow my knees before the Father, from whom every family in heaven and on earth derives its name, that He would grant you, according to the riches of His glory, to be strengthened with power through His Spirit in the inner man, so that Christ may dwell in your hearts through faith; and that you, being rooted and grounded in love, may be able to comprehend with all the saints what is the breadth and length and height and depth, and to know the love of Christ which surpasses knowledge, that you may be filled up to all the fullness of God. Now to Him who is able to do far more abundantly beyond all that we ask or think, according to the power that works within us, to Him be the glory in the church and in Christ Jesus to all generations forever and ever. Amen.*

Jesus knew that without His presence, the disciples would soon fall away. He warned them this would happen in the immediate aftermath of His arrest (Matthew 26:31); Peter proclaimed his loyalty, but without the abiding comfort and strength of the beloved Savior, he quickly succumbed to fear and denied Christ (John 18:25-27).

We need the strength of the abiding Christ to make it in this life; this strength has been made available through the precious Holy Spirit, a gift from Jesus.

John 16:7 – *But I tell you the truth, it is to your advantage that I go away; for if I do not go away, the Helper will not come to you; but if I go, I will send Him to you.*

Paul knew from personal experience what it was to be passionately religious, fervent even, for the things of God, but without the Spirit of God. In his own strength, he pursued what he thought was pleasing to God, but was in fact diametrically opposed to the One he claimed to serve. Jesus interrupted his life on the road to Damascus, blinded him, and after three days sent him to Ananias who laid hands on him and gave him the message that God had called him to take the gospel to the Gentiles. As a result, the scales fell from his eyes, and Paul regained his sight and was filled with the Holy Spirit (Acts 9:17-18).

What a difference this made! Paul went from persecuting the church to pastoring its people and preaching the gospel. He stopped doing life in his own strength and was empowered and strengthened by the divine power of God. The Holy Spirit would sustain him through much suffering and persecution, afflictions, dangers, and distresses of all kinds, both mental, emotional, and physical.

Jesus never meant for you and I to live the Christian life in our own strength. This is why Paul prays for the Ephesian believers to be *strengthened with power through His Spirit in the inner man.*

The Holy Spirit does many things for us; after all, He is God Himself, coming to take up residence in the immaterial, spiritual part of us that is able to commune with God. He is given to us as a gift, a pledge of what God has promised us in eternity (Ephesians 1:13-14). Jesus calls us His bride. At the moment of salvation, we are betrothed, or engaged to Him, awaiting our marriage which will take place in the future when the body of Christ is taken up to be with Him in heaven. There will be a "marriage supper of the Lamb" (Revelation 19:7-9) when we are finally united with Christ and our physical bodies are redeemed.

In the meantime, the Holy Spirit is a promise, as when a bridegroom gives his future bride an engagement ring. It's a taste of what's to come, a guarantee that He intends to carry through and honor the covenant He has made with us in salvation. The indwelling presence of the Holy Spirit helps us *comprehend with all the saints what is the breadth and length and height and depth and to know the love of Christ,* our bridegroom.

We are never without Christ.
We are never alone.
We are never left to live this life in our own strength.

God is able to do more abundantly [through us, in us, and for us] beyond all that we ask or think *according to the power that works within us.* This power is the mighty, amazing, resurrecting power of the Holy Spirit, the same Spirit that raised Christ from the dead (Romans 8:11).

When you start to think you are alone, think again. If you belong to Christ, the Holy Spirit is in you, and all the strength you need is available. Stop trying to live a spiritual life by physical means and learn to walk in the strength of the Spirit. Jesus gave you all you need when He gave you His Spirit.

Philippians 4:13 – *I can do all things through Him who strengthens me.*

Pray Today

Dear Jesus, Thank You for the gift of the Holy Spirit. Your abiding presence in our hearts and minds continually fills us up. We know You love us; we feel Your strength; and Your presence in Spirit makes us long to know You in completeness. One day, our bodies will be redeemed, and we will be able to dwell with You physically, face to face. Until then, teach us to walk in Your Spirit, to hear Your voice, and to allow You to strengthen us for each day's challenges. Help us to be Spirit-filled people who are faithful to the gospel because we are strengthened by You. Amen.

DAY 26: THE GIFT OF SECURITY

If the Lord be with us, we have no cause of fear.
His eye is upon us, His arm over us,
His ear open to our prayer, His grace sufficient,
His promise unchangeable.
–John Newton

Psalm 121:7 – *The Lord will protect you from all evil; He will keep your soul.*

Jesus came to do away with insecurity and fear, to strengthen us for this life. Fear has been defined as *an unpleasant often strong emotion caused by anticipation or awareness of danger* (Merriman-Webster). Insecurity comes when we are ruled by our fears; our anxiety takes root. This causes us to be unstable and shaky in our faith walk, distracts us from our mission and purpose as believers, and causes us to miss out on many of the blessings God intends us to enjoy.

I believe there are two main areas where believers struggle with fear. Jesus came to give us the gift of security in both.

#1 – The fear of losing our salvation.

1 Peter 1:3-5 – *Blessed be the God and Father of our Lord Jesus Christ, who according to His great mercy has caused us to be born again to a living hope through the resurrection of Jesus Christ from the dead, to obtain an inheritance which is imperishable and undefiled and will not fade away, reserved in heaven for you, who are protected by the power of God through faith for a salvation ready to be revealed in the last time.*

God is the initiator of your salvation, Jesus provided what was necessary to accomplish it, and the Holy Spirit sustains you in it. You did nothing to accomplish redemption; you simply responded to what God did when He tugged on your heart, opened your spiritual eyes, and showed you who He is.

We begin our relationship with God by faith in what He has done, and we trust Him to complete the work He began (Philippians 1:6). Our obedience and faithfulness to God does not sustain our salvation; it is simply evidence that salvation exists. Jesus says that it is He who gives eternal life to His sheep, and *they will never perish; and no one will snatch them out of My hand. My Father, who has given them to Me, is greater than all; and no one is able to snatch them out of the Father's hand* (John 10:28-29).

How do we persevere and keep from falling away? We allow the Holy Spirit to do His work in us. Those who fall away do not lose their salvation. In scripture, "falling away" is always in context of unbelief. Those who appear to have once believed, but turn away from God when persecution or hardship occurs, reveal they did not believe unto salvation. Fear not! If you have truly placed your faith in Christ, you will make it home to heaven.

#2 – The fear of physical harm.

2 Thessalonians 3:3 – *But the Lord is faithful, and He will strengthen and protect you from the evil one.*

2 Timothy 4:16-18 – *At my first defense no one supported me, but all deserted me; may it not be counted against them. But the Lord stood with me and strengthened me, so that through me the proclamation might be fully accomplished, and that all the Gentiles might hear; and I was rescued out of the lion's mouth. The Lord will rescue me from every evil deed, and will bring me safely to His heavenly kingdom; to Him be the glory forever and ever. Amen.*

God's promises to protect us does not mean that we will never suffer physical harm, sickness, disease, or injury. We live in a fallen world. What it does mean is that nothing happens outside God's permission, and that if He allows harm to come, it is for our good and His glory. God has already defeated the ultimate harm that all of us fear: *death.* In defeating death, God has taken away all fear. In fact, what the world sees as the worst thing that can happen is actually the best thing for those who know Christ. Death is simply a door to meet Jesus face to face.

Paul faced many hardships. I'm sure there were times when his heart raced, and his knees trembled in anticipation of what might happen to him physically. No one likes pain and suffering. Yet, he was fully confident that God would protect and preserve his life until the day he finished the course God planned for him. He knew his days were ordained by a sovereign God (Psalm 139:16); he had opened the gift of security and knew that God would bring him safely home.

Psalm 91:1-2 – *He who dwells in the shelter of the Most High will abide in the shadow of the Almighty. I will say to the Lord, "My refuge and my fortress, my God, in whom I trust!"*

Pray Today

Dear Jesus, Thank You for the gift of security. There are so many promises in Your Word of Your protecting and sustaining grace. You have armies of angels that stand ready to battle on our behalf at Your command. We can trust You to protect us, just as we have trusted You to secure our eternal salvation. Thank You that insecurity has no place in the lives of those who meet You. Amen.

DAY 27: THE GIFT OF COURAGE

Courage is contagious.
When a brave man takes a stand, the spines of others are often stiffened.
—Billy Graham

Isaiah 35:4 – *Say to those with anxious heart, "Take courage, fear not. Behold, your God will come with vengeance; the recompense of God will come, but He will save you."*

The Old Testament Hebrew word translated as *take courage* is *chazaq*. It means to hold fast, to strengthen, to make firm. The phrase is translated *be strong* in the King James Version. Courage and strength are intimately connected and describe the same response to adversity. The source of our strength is directly relative to the kind of courage we are able to exhibit.

How do we "take courage?" How do we take hold of the strength of the Lord?

Courage comes when we put our hope in the Lord.
Psalm 27:14 – *Wait for the Lord; Be strong and let your heart take courage; Yes, wait for the Lord.*

This word *wait* in this verse means to wait with expectation and hope and is also used in the context of binding together or joining. You may have heard the phrase, "hitch your wagon to a star," meaning to pursue success by partnering with someone who is already there. As Christ-followers, we are joined to Christ; we can set our hopes on Him, and gain courage from knowing He has already conquered every foe, defeated every temptation, and guaranteed our triumphant entrance into heaven. We can *be strong and let [our] heart take courage*, because we are those who *hope in the Lord* (Psalm 31:24). We take hold of the Lord, and He strengthens us by His hold on us.

Courage comes when we experience the peace of Jesus.
John 16:33 – *These things I have spoken to you, so that in Me you may have peace. In the world you have tribulation, but take courage; I have overcome the world."*

Peace is the absence of hostility. For the Christ-follower, peace is defined as *the tranquil state of a soul assured of its salvation through Christ, and so fearing nothing from God and content with its earthly lot, of whatsoever sort that is.*[23] In Christ, we have peace *with* God, having all accounts settled and our sins forgiven; this gives us the peace *of* God that calms our anxious thoughts as we abide in Christ. Just before Jesus said these words, He reminded us that we are the branches who must remain in the vine, for apart from Him we can do nothing (John 15:5).

Courage comes from the promise of the Holy Spirit.
2 Corinthians 5:5-7 – *Now He who prepared us for this very purpose is God, who gave to us the Spirit as a pledge. Therefore, being always of good courage, and knowing that while we are at home in the body we are absent from the Lord— for we walk by faith, not by sight.*

The Spirit of God is God's promise that all things turn out well for us in the end, and that He will finish our redemption story. Knowing what awaits us on the other side of this life gives us courage to face death with anticipation, not fear.

Courage comes from the perseverance of the Scriptures.
Romans 15:4-5 – *For whatever was written in earlier times was written for our instruction, so that through perseverance and the encouragement of the Scriptures we might have hope. Now may the God who gives perseverance and encourage-ment grant you to be of the same mind with one another according to Christ Jesus.*

I'll let you in on a secret. Whenever I face something that is completely beyond my abilities, I remind myself that many others have faced similar circumstances, and they survived. Scripture is filled with the stories of God's faithful preservation and protection of His people. A deep and abiding conviction that God's Word is absolutely true is a bottomless well of truth from which we can draw all the necessary courage to strengthen our faith and walk.

Courage comes from the presence of the saints.
1 Thessalonians 5:11,14 – *Therefore encourage one another and build up one another, just as you also are doing. We urge you, brethren, admonish the unruly, encourage the fainthearted, help the weak, be patient with everyone.*

In his search for meaning and purpose in life, Solomon learned it's never good to go at life alone. He warns, *Woe to the one who falls when there is not another to lift him up* and reminds us that *a cord of three strands is not quickly torn apart* (Ecclesiastes 4:10b,12b). The gift of courage often comes through the encouragement of other believers. Sharing our fears and anxieties with a trusted friend opens the door to receive the courageous news that God will see us through, and we are not alone in our journey.

Do you need courage? Put your hope in Jesus and find your strength in Him.

Pray Today

Dear Jesus, Thank You for the gift of courage. Your Word, Your people, Your promises, and Your presence is all we need to face our fears, no matter what. Teach us to lean on You for the strength and courage we need to take heart in the face of every discouragement. Amen.

DAY 28: THE GIFT OF TRIALS

Why should I tremble at the plow of my Lord
that makes deep furrows on my soul?
For He is no idle husbandman, He purposes a crop.
—Samuel Rutherford

James 1:2-4 – *Consider it all joy, my brethren, when you encounter various trials, knowing that the testing of your faith produces endurance. And let endurance have its perfect result, so that you may be perfect and complete, lacking in nothing.*

God is the ultimate personal trainer in spiritual matters. James tells us count it all joy when we **encounter** various trials. The word translated *encounter* is *peripiptō*; its literal meaning is to "fall into" so that one is "surrounded." It's used two other times in the New Testament. In the story of the Good Samaritan, the man "fell among" thieves; and when Paul's ship ran aground, it "fell among" the place where two seas met. You get the idea. Trials are the times we find ourselves in circumstances we are unable to control, and that take over our lives, pushing us in a direction we didn't want to go.

How comforting to know that God is sovereign and directs our steps (Proverbs 16:9). While we might not "see it coming" God is perfectly aware and sovereignly involved in managing the daily minutiae of our lives to engage us in His spiritual personal training exercises.

How do trials strengthen us? We only need to look at our physical bodies for the answer. Medical science has discovered the secret of building muscle. Before we can grow strong, we must be torn down. The repeated breaking down of the muscles by repetitive lifting, followed by periods of restorative rest, causes our muscles to grow both in size and strength.

Muscle size increases when a person continually challenges the muscles to deal with higher levels of resistance or weight. This process is known as muscle hypertrophy. Muscle hypertrophy occurs when the fibers of the muscles sustain damage or injury. The body repairs damaged fibers by fusing them, which increases the mass and size of the muscles.[22]

The medical term, *hypertrophy* comes from Latin, and has a literal meaning of "over" [*hyper*] and "the defeat of an enemy" [*trophy*]. We need spiritual hypertrophy – God's gift of trials that defeat the inherent sinful tendencies that keep our faith weak and build up our spiritual muscles with His strength. We can't just walk into the gym of life and take on the heavy lifting in the same way a person who has been faithfully working out spiritually for a lifetime! We admire those "spiritually fit" people for their strong faith, godly wisdom, passionate love, and loyalty to God. They have paid the price of spiritual growth: persevering in trials, endurance in suffering, faithful obedience, self-denial, and studying and emulating the words and actions of our Master Trainer, Jesus.

James tells us we will encounter **various** trials. This word is also translated "diverse" or "manifold." God is a *personal* trainer; while we face similar struggles since we are all casualties of the human condition called *sin*, I believe God is quite personal when it comes to the nature of our training program. Some things that really bother you might not be an issue for me. God knows exactly what we need in our lives to develop our spiritual muscles.

Other uses of the word *various* give us an idea of the kinds of trials that God may allow to come our way. God does not tempt us to sin, but He does test. Trials may consist of various kinds of sickness and disease (Matthew 4:24, Mark 1:34, Luke 4:40), various kinds of lusts (2 Timothy 3:6, Titus 3:3), or various kinds of strange doctrines (Hebrews 13:9). Can you see the implications? Trials work to discipline and strengthen us physically, mentally, and emotionally, as well as spiritually.

Here's the good news. God also has *manifold grace* for every trial. Peter encourages believers to use their gifts to serve one another as *good stewards of the manifold grace of God* (1 Peter 4:10). Manifold is the same word as various, which tells us that God is quite able to provide exactly what is needed for us to be victorious in our trials.

What trials are you facing? Do you see your struggles as something to get out of as quickly as possible, or will you accept them as one of the gifts of belonging to Jesus? Will you allow your trials to accomplish the greater purpose God intends to work out in you?

1 Peter 1:6-7 – *In this you greatly rejoice, even though now for a little while, if necessary, you have been distressed by various trials, so that the proof of your faith, being more precious than gold which is perishable, even though tested by fire, may be found to result in praise and glory and honor at the revelation of Jesus Christ.*

Pray Today

Dear Jesus, Thank You for the gift of trials. While we open this gift with fear and trembling, we know each trial is personally selected by the Father with an eternal purpose in mind. Let us be faithful in the spiritual gym of life and welcome Your training exercises. May our minds and hearts be strengthened as we persevere, and may Your image be formed in us, for Your glory. Amen.

DAY 29: THE GIFT OF PRAYER

It is good to be conscious that we are always in the presence of God.
It is better to gaze upon Him in adoration.
But it is best of all to commune with Him as a Friend — and that is prayer.
—Unknown[24]

Luke 11:1-4 – *It happened that while Jesus was praying in a certain place, after He had finished, one of his disciples said to Him, "Lord, teach us to pray just as John also taught his disciples." And He said to them, "When you pray, say: 'Father, hallowed be Your name. Your kingdom come. Give us each day our daily bread. And forgive us our sins, for we ourselves also forgive everyone who is indebted to us. And lead us not into temptation.'"*

Suppose you have a great need which can only be met by one person in the universe. This person is enormously powerful, extremely wealthy, and incredibly wise, and known to have great influence and authority over all things. In order to have your need met, you must go to this person and ask for what you need, but you have no idea how to approach him or what to say to him. Fortunately, you have a close friend who knows this person very intimately; in fact, he is his son. Wouldn't it be prudent to consult your good friend on how to approach his father?

This was the situation in which the disciples found themselves. They recognized they needed a personal relationship with God, and that Jesus was the only one able to show them the way. Wisely, they asked him, *Teach us to pray.*

Both Matthew and Luke record Jesus' lesson on prayer. Perhaps Matthew was the more auditory learner (or he took better notes); he expands on Luke's version (Matthew 6:9-13). In both passages, Jesus demonstrates four simple principles of how to approach His Father in prayer so that we grow stronger in our relationship with God and more effective in the work He is doing in and through us.

Pray with a humble heart.
Hallowed be Your name, Your kingdom come.

Prayer begins with acknowledging who God is. His name is *hallowed*, set apart, holy. We approach God's presence with humility, recognizing the price Jesus paid to give us entrance into His throne room. We come with a desire not for our will, but for God's kingdom to be established in our world. At the moment of Jesus' crucifixion, the temple veil was torn in two from top to bottom, symbolizing that God had opened the door wide into the Holy of Holies, the place where His presence dwelled over the mercy seat (Matthew 27:51, Exodus

25:22). Up until that day, no man could enter the Holy of Holies except the high priest, and then only once a year and only with the blood of a sacrificed animal. It was a serious and holy thing to approach God! The priest even wore bells on his robe and a rope around his leg so that if God struck him dead, his fellow priests could pull him out.

Pray with a dependent heart.
Give us each day our daily bread.

The Father knows our need before we ask Him (Matthew 6:8,32). Yet, He wants us to verbalize our need, expressing that we are totally dependent on Him to provide. The phrase *daily bread* indicates a request for what God knows is necessary to strengthen us physically, spiritually, mentally, and emotionally. It is not a wish list of self-centered, material comforts.

Pray with a clean heart.
Forgive us our sins, for we ourselves also forgive.

God does not hear our prayers if we hold sin in our hearts (Psalm 66:18). God desires we lift up holy hands (Psalm 28:2) and approach Him with a heart ready to confess our own sins and forgive others for their wrongs against us because we have been forgiven (Ephesians 4:32).

Pray with an alert heart.
Lead us not into temptation [but deliver us from evil].

We have an adversary that walks about as a roaring lion, looking to devour us (1 Peter 5:8). Jesus later admonished the disciples to "watch and pray" to avoid temptation (Mark 14:38), and Paul taught the believers to "be alert" in their prayers (Ephesians 6:18, Colossians 4:2). We are to pray with an awareness of the enemy's schemes to distract us, seeking God's wisdom, power, and direction to walk *away* from the temptations of this life.

Jesus gave us a gift; He made it possible for us to come into God's presence, and then taught us how to do it in both word and example. His disciples recognized the strength Jesus gained from spending time in fellowship and prayer with His Father. Come to the Father in humility and dependence with a clean heart, alert to the distractions that will keep you from opening the gift of prayer.

Pray Today

Dear Jesus, Thank You for opening the door to the Father's throne room. Because of You, we are welcomed and encouraged to spend time there, worshipping the One who provides all our needs. What great joy it is to know that God desires us to draw near to Him, to enjoy His presence and find our soul's satisfaction and strength. Amen.

76

SUSTAINING GIFTS
Day 30 – Day 36

Cast your burden upon the Lord and He will sustain you;
He will never allow the righteous to be shaken.
Psalm 55:22

Jesus came to give us what we need to sustain us in this life.
He knows the world we live in.
He came in the flesh, lived as a man just like you and me.
He knows how to provide for His people.
He understands we need rest and peace to face each day.
He loves us unconditionally and brings joy in every circumstance.
His presence gives us hope we can navigate this fallen world,
and He is there to comfort us when life is simply too hard to manage.

DAY 30: THE GIFT OF PROVISION

When God provides more money, we often think, "this is a blessing."
Well, yes, but it would be just as scriptural to think, "this is a test."
—Randy Alcorn[25]

Philippians 4:19 – *And my God will supply all your needs according to His riches in glory in Christ Jesus.*

In the world's eyes, one who amasses a great deal of money is generally held up as a successful person. We are a culture who worships material possessions, and our desire for *more* is never satisfied. Those who have received Christ have a different view of life; money and possessions aren't things to be gained, but rather tools to steward for God's kingdom.

God promised many times to provide all that is needed to sustain our lives. He is an attentive Father, seeing to the needs of His family. He is able to provide not only our physical needs, but the spiritual, emotional, and mental requirements for daily living. In Christ, we have **all** we need.

Here are three principles of God's economy by which He fulfills His promise to supply all our needs.

Prioritize the Kingdom.
Matthew 6:8,31-33 – *Your Father knows what you need before you ask Him. Do not worry then, saying, 'What will we eat?' or 'What will we drink?' or 'What will we wear for clothing?' For the Gentiles eagerly seek all these things; for your heavenly Father knows that you need all these things. But seek first His kingdom and His righteousness, and all these things will be added to you.*

Our earthly lives are simply a scaffolding on which to carry out kingdom business. In a very real sense, we are employees of Jesus. Once we come to Christ, we become physical representatives of a spiritual world that exists outside the knowledge and understanding of those who have not met the Savior. We are His ambassadors, sent out into the world to invite others in. As our children's pastor used to explain, *God is the boss of us*, and He is responsible to provide everything necessary for the work He has given us to do.

This is not to say we do not hold jobs or pursue careers. We do not park ourselves on the couch and expect God to have take-out delivered. God is at work in us, giving us the desires, talents, and abilities to carry out a myriad of different kinds of work in this world, but our physical work is the framework on which kingdom work is accomplished. Our goal is not to build a successful career; it is to seek His kingdom first and foremost, and to live righteous lives that are a magnet and an example to others of the goodness of God. We focus on the kingdom, trusting God to provide all that is needed to accomplish His work.

Give generously.
2 Corinthians 9:6-8 – *Now this I say, he who sows sparingly will also reap sparingly, and he who sows bountifully will also reap bountifully. Each one must do just as he has purposed in his heart, not grudgingly or under compulsion, for God loves a cheerful giver. And God is able to make all grace abound to you, so that always having a sufficiency in everything, you may have an abundance for every good deed.*

The world teaches us to take care of our own needs first before we think about giving anything away. We tend to give out of our abundance, but God tells us to give not sparingly, but bountifully, trusting that He will take care of our needs. Paul commends the believers for their sacrificial giving to meet the needs of the whole body of Christ and reminds them that this type of giving results in "profit which increases to your account" (Philippians 4:17). The most generous people aren't necessarily those who have the most money; generous people are simply those who realize their blessings are a responsibility to steward for the good of the body and the growth of the kingdom.

Work hard to help others.
Ephesians 4:28 – *He who steals must steal no longer; but rather he must labor, performing with his own hands what is good, so that he will have something to share with one who has need.*

In God's economy, those who have the ability to work and earn should also be involved in helping the poor. Jesus concerned Himself with our needs. We are all spiritually destitute and unable to get ourselves out of the predicament of the poverty of our sinful condition. We should look at those in need and see ourselves and do for them what we would desire others to do for us. This is one of the distinguishing marks of a true believer (1 John 3:17).

Have you received the gift of God's sustaining provision? Trust Him to continue to provide as you center your life on Christ and His kingdom, share generously, and work hard to meet the needs of others.

It's not what you do with the million if fortune should ere be your lot, but what are you doing at present with the dollar and quarter you got. (Copied)

Pray Today

Dear Jesus, Thank You for sustaining my life with abundance which meets all my needs. I can trust You to continue to provide. Your resources are unlimited, and You are a kind and generous God. Teach me to steward every blessing for Your kingdom. Amen.

DAY 31: THE GIFT OF REST

How many of our sleepless hours might be traced
to our untrusting and disordered minds.
They slumber sweetly whom faith rocks to sleep.
No pillow so soft as a promise; no coverlet so warm
as an assured interest in Christ.
—Charles Spurgeon[26]

Psalm 3:5; 4:8 – *I lay down and slept; I awoke, for the Lord sustains me. ... In peace I will both lie down and sleep, for You alone, O Lord, make me to dwell in safety.*

Rest was an original gift bestowed in the Garden of Eden. God set the example when He created the world in six days and rested on the seventh. Long before Moses was handed a tablet with the Sabbath directive inscribed upon it, *God blessed the seventh day and sanctified it, because in it He rested from all His work which God had created and made* (Genesis 2:3).

Our physical bodies are made to need regular rest. God created us with the ability to sleep, something which scientists and medical professionals still study and have yet to completely understand. Our central nervous systems are able to shut themselves down in some miraculous fashion, allowing the mind and body to rest and restore itself. Daily sleep is necessary for our bodies to function properly; in the same way, spiritual rest is essential for our soul and spirit. We crave rest from the burdens of living in an unredeemed world, the battles with our flesh, and the worries and concerns of our lives.

Jesus came to give us both physical and spiritual rest as we surrender our lives to Him in faithful obedience, trusting Him to get us home.

Our hearts rest as we are joined to Jesus in salvation.
Matthew 11:28-29 – *Come to Me, all who are weary and heavy-laden, and I will give you rest. Take My yoke upon you and learn from Me, for I am gentle and humble in heart, and you will find rest for your souls.*

Salvation is the beginning (and only source) of true rest. We are weary from trying to manage life on our own terms and heavy-laden with our sins. Jesus removes our yoke of sin and brings us into a relationship with Himself. We find Him to be gentle and humble, a loving Savior who bears the load for us as we walk in step with Him. Only then can our hearts be fully at rest.

Our minds rest as we wait on Jesus.
Psalm 37:7 – *Rest in the Lord and wait patiently for Him; do not fret because of him who prospers in his way, because of the man who carries out wicked schemes.*

Worry steals our rest. We fret and stew over things we can't control or change. A mind at rest has learned the secret of giving over our frustrations and anxieties to the only One who can do anything about them. We rest in God's justice; we wait patiently for Him to make all things right.

Our souls rest in obedience to Jesus.
Jeremiah 6:16 – *Thus says the Lord, "Stand by the ways and see and ask for the ancient paths, where the good way is, and walk in it; and you will find rest for your souls." But they said, "We will not walk in it."*

Disobedience to God's commands wreaks havoc on our emotions. Can you lay your head down on your pillow at night and know that you are at peace with your Creator? A guilty conscience won't be silenced. The way to rest is confession of sin, receiving God's forgiveness, and changing our ways to obey Him. We may think we are getting away with breaking God's commands, but our souls will not rest while we continue in disobedience.

Our bodies rest in trusting Jesus.
Proverbs 19:23 – *The fear of the Lord leads to life, so that one may sleep satisfied, untouched by evil.*

The fear of the Lord is living in light of who God is, reverencing and respecting His ways, and trusting Him with our lives. A proper fear of God causes us not to fear anything else, allowing our bodies to rest in full confidence that He will protect us from all evil.

Our spirits rest in being with Jesus.
Hebrews 4:9-10 – *So there remains a Sabbath rest for the people of God. For the one who has entered His rest has himself also rested from his works, as God did from His.*

One day we will enter into our final Sabbath rest, eternity in the presence of God. No more sin. No more pain. No more tears. No more battles. No more worries. No more anxiety. No more sleepless nights. In fact, we won't need sleep at all, because we will exist in a complete state of rest, at home with Jesus.

Have you opened the gift of rest or are you still worrying and losing sleep over things you can't control? Be yoked with Jesus and walk with Him. Trust Him. Obey Him. And get some rest.

Pray Today

Dear Jesus, Thank You for the gift of rest. Thank You that we do not have to lie awake at night with our minds full of worry and get up the next day more tired than when we lay down. You give us spiritual rest for our souls and physical rest for our bodies. Help us to trust You and rest. Amen.

DAY 32: THE GIFT OF PEACE

[Peace] is the deep, settled confidence that all is well between the soul and
God because of His loving, sovereign control of one's life both in time and
eternity. That calm assurance is based on the knowledge that sins are forgiven,
blessing is present, good is abundant even in trouble, and heaven is ahead.
–John MacArthur[27]

Psalm 29:11 – *The Lord will give strength to His people; the Lord will bless His people with peace.*

Where is the place you feel the most at peace? For many people, when they imagine a peaceful scenario, they think of a garden. Spending time in a well-tended garden filled with beautiful plants, water features and walking paths calms their soul. Shady corners under leafy trees and a comfortable bench for getting lost in one's thoughts is a welcome and peaceful escape from our chaotic and noisy world. Did you ever wonder why?

Life began in a garden. God designed the perfect landscape and then created us to find great peace and satisfaction in it. The relationship between Adam and Eve and God was originally the *deep, settled confidence that all is well between the soul and God,* as described by John MacArthur in the above quote.

Sin destroyed our peace, but Jesus came as the Prince of Peace to restore it. He came to give us entrance back to the garden where God wanted us to live.

The gift of peace is particularly unique among those who have found faith in Christ and is a distinguishing characteristic of Spirit-filled believers. In the Old Testament, the Hebrew word *shalowm* is rooted in the idea of wholeness, or completeness. In the New Testament, the Greek word is *eirēnē,* meaning a state of tranquility as the opposite of war and dissension.

We have peace *with* God because He has abolished the sin which separated us. Before Christ, we are considered enemies of God (Romans 5:10). Jesus came to bring peace with God (Romans 5:1). The war has been won; Jesus signed the peace treaty with His own blood on the cross.

Ephesians 2:13-16 – *But now in Christ Jesus you who formerly were far off have been brought near by the blood of Christ. For He Himself is our peace, who made both groups into one and broke down the barrier of the dividing wall, by abolishing in His flesh the enmity, which is the Law of commandments contained in ordinances, so that in Himself He might make the two into one new man, thus establishing peace, and might reconcile them both in one body to God through the cross, by it having put to death the enmity.*

We have the peace *of* God because we are made whole in Jesus, restored back to our original creation, and indwelt by the Holy Spirit. Peace is a fruit of the Spirit (Galatians 5:22); His presence in us brings the peace Jesus promised before He went to the cross.

John 14:27 – *Peace I leave with you; My peace I give to you; not as the world gives do I give to you. Do not let your heart be troubled, nor let it be fearful.*

Peace is a state of being, but it manifests itself in our thoughts and emotions. According to scripture, it's a decision of the heart and mind to live in peace.

Romans 8:6 – *For the mind set on the flesh is death, but the mind set on the Spirit is life and peace.*

We choose what we want to think about. If we spend hours taking in a steady diet of worldly thinking and spend little time thinking about the things of God, we will have little peace. We can set our minds on the Spirit by reading God's Word and other books that inspire and teach us about our faith, listening to music that worships and honors God, memorizing scripture, and talking to God throughout the day.

In four short verses, Paul revealed the secret of a peace-filled life to the Philippian believers. A grateful heart changes our perspective and allows us to sincerely pray about our needs, moving the burden from our shoulders to God's. As we make intentional decisions about what to allow our thoughts to dwell on (true, right, honorable, excellent, pure, lovely, etc.), our mindset moves from anxiousness to peace.

Philippians 4:6-7,9 – *Be anxious for nothing, but in everything by prayer and supplication with thanksgiving let your requests be made known to God. And the peace of God, which surpasses all comprehension, will guard your hearts and your minds in Christ Jesus. ... The things you have learned and received and heard and seen in me, practice these things, and the God of peace will be with you.*

Don't make the mistake of thinking an earthly, man-made garden can bring the peace for which your soul longs. Real peace is encountering everlasting peace *with* God and learning to walk in the peace *of* God. Real peace is a gift only Jesus can give.

Pray Today

Dear Jesus, Thank You for peace. In this noisy, chaotic, and often-scary world, we long for the peace that only comes through a relationship with You. Help us never to settle for the imitation the world offers, but to enjoy a life of peace as we walk with You today, in anticipation of eternal peace when we are once again back in the Garden with You. Amen.

DAY 33: THE GIFT OF HOPE

Hope, from a biblical perspective,
is a future certainty grounded in a present reality.
–Victor Shepherd[28]

Romans 8:23-25 – *And not only this, but also we ourselves, having the first fruits of the Spirit, even we ourselves groan within ourselves, waiting eagerly for our adoption as sons, the redemption of our body. For in hope we have been saved, but hope that is seen is not hope; for who hopes for what he already sees? But if we hope for what we do not see, with perseverance we wait eagerly for it.*

Hope is defined as a joyful, confident expectation or anticipation. It is to have a desire for something accompanied by belief in fulfillment. It is human nature to be hopeful, to anticipate things will get better or that the desires of our hearts will be met.

Before we meet Jesus, we can only place our hope in things that will most certainly disappoint us. The world has a bad habit of letting us down. Relationships we thought would last forever are dissolved. People get sick and die. The company we thought we would retire from goes bankrupt. The stock market crashes, and our 401k is depleted. We find out termites have destroyed the foundation of our dream home.

Many people *hope* for heaven. They measure themselves against others, hoping that if there is an afterlife, they will make the grade and be allowed to enjoy it. Sadly, some people have given up on hoping for heaven. With no experience of heavenly things to persuade them of its reality, they are *hopeless.*

Hope is only as good as the object of our hope. Jesus came to give us a sure and steadfast hope that will sustain us until it is fulfilled. Our hope is not some "pie-in-the-sky" dream. It is rooted in actual events that create a tangible anticipation and expectation; what Jesus began, He will complete.

In Jesus, we hope for many things.

We hope to see the glory of God (Romans 5:2).
We hope for the created world to be set free from the curse (Romans 8:20-21).
We hope for our physical bodies to be fully redeemed (Romans 8:23).
We hope for Christ to be exalted through our lives (Philippians 1:20).
We hope to be resurrected when we die (1 Thessalonians 4:13).
We hope for Jesus' return (Titus 2:13).
We hope for eternal life (Titus 1:2; 3:7).

We hope to see Jesus and be made like Him (1 John 3:2-3).
We hope for heaven (Colossians 1:5).

Our hope is rooted in the work Jesus did on the cross and the Father's confirmation of that work in raising Jesus from the dead. Jesus has already done the impossible. He has paid our sin debt, opening the door to having all our hopes fulfilled. He defeated death, the last enemy standing in the way of our hopes for eternal life.

Hebrews 6:18-20a – *So that by two unchangeable things in which it is impossible for God to lie, we who have taken refuge would have strong encouragement to take hold of the hope set before us. This hope we have as an anchor of the soul, a hope both sure and steadfast and one which enters the veil, where Jesus has entered as a forerunner for us.*

The Holy Spirit came to indwell followers of Jesus, allowing us a taste of what it will be like when we no longer *hope* for what God has promised us, but actually experience those promises in all their fullness (Romans 8:23-25).

God wants us to have hope. He created us with desires that cannot be met in this world. Jesus came to give us the gift of a strong and steadfast hope upon which we can build our lives. To hope in God is not a weak and fading wish for a better life. Our hope is a practical, tangible, confident assurance based on God's actions. Every day we wake up we are one day closer to seeing all our hopes fulfilled, because we are one day closer to being face to face with the One in whom those hopes are set.

Have you opened the gift of hope? Don't spend one more day thinking God's promises will never come true. Set your anchor deep in the sure and steadfast hope that Jesus came to give us.

Romans 15:13 – *Now may the God of hope fill you with all joy and peace in believing, so that you will abound in hope by the power of the Holy Spirit.*

Pray Today

Dear Jesus, Thank You for the gift of hope. Our hopes are not simply wishes or dreams, as they were before we met You. Our hope is a confident expectation that what You promised is already "as good as done." Your Word is filled with descriptions of all that is ahead for those who love You and belong to Your kingdom. Teach us to be hopeful, to live hopeful lives, and to speak of the hope we have in You. We live in a world of people without hope; let us be faithful messengers of the hope of the gospel until all things are fulfilled in Your presence. Amen.

DAY 34: THE GIFT OF LOVE

Christ died not in order to make God love us,
but because He did love His people.
Calvary is the supreme demonstration of Divine love.
Whenever you are tempted to doubt the love of God, go back to Calvary.
—A.W. Pink[29]

The love of God is the motivating force behind all His interactions with us. We were created out of the love of God's own heart, intimately and intentionally designed to receive His love, return that love to Him, and live in such a way that love overflows to others. Love is an attribute of God; it is one of His inherent character traits. God is love, and so every action and thought that originates with God is one of love.

Jesus came into our world to manifest God's love, or to make it visible (1 John 4:9). He is the tangible expression of God's personal love for His people. Love has many definitions, but ultimately, it is an act of the will that has as its motivation the good of the one loved. We can know and understand God's heart of love by observing *how* He loved.

God's love is an inclusive love.
John 3:16 – *For God so loved the world, that He gave His only begotten Son, that whoever believes in Him shall not perish, but have eternal life.*

Human love is limited; we tend to love those who love us. In contrast, God loves all people. Jesus came so that everyone has the opportunity to gain eternal life through belief in Him. God includes everyone, but not everyone accepts the love God offers.

God's love is a saving love.
Ephesians 2:4-5 – *But God, being rich in mercy, because of His great love with which He loved us, even when we were dead in our transgressions, made us alive together with Christ (by grace you have been saved).*

God's love for us moved Him to act. He extended mercy and grace, sending Jesus to take care of our sin problem so that we could be saved. God's love saw a need and acted to meet that need. He loved us, so He saved us.

God's love is a committed love.
Romans 8:38-39 – *For I am convinced that neither death, nor life, nor angels, nor principalities, nor things present, nor things to come, nor powers, nor height, nor depth, nor any other created thing, will be able to separate us from the love of God, which is in Christ Jesus our Lord.*

God is a covenant-keeping God. When He sets His love on us, it is forever. We can disappoint and grieve God, we can disobey God, and we can love other things more than we love God. But we can never do anything to cause Him to stop loving us, or to love us less.

God's love is a sacrificial love.
Romans 5:8 – *But God demonstrates His own love toward us, in that while we were yet sinners, Christ died for us.*

Real love sacrifices even to the point of death. Jesus's death for sinners was the greatest act of unselfish, sacrificial love ever known to mankind.

God's love is a fatherly love.
1 John 3:1a – *See how great a love the Father has bestowed on us, that we would be called children of God; and such we are.*

God loves us as a Father loves His children. We are adopted into the family, counted as sons and daughters, and co-heirs with Jesus (Romans 8:15,17).

God's love is a personal love.
John 14:21 – *He who has My commandments and keeps them is the one who loves Me; and he who loves Me will be loved by My Father, and I will love him and will disclose Myself to him.*

When we accept Jesus' love, and love Him in return, we enter into a unique relationship. Jesus reveals Himself to us and we are loved in a personal and intimate way as we experience His indwelling Spirit.

God's love is a supernatural love.
John 15:9 – *Just as the Father has loved Me, I have also loved you; abide in My love.*

Jesus loves us with the same kind of love that exists between Him and His Father. It is a perfect, eternal love, and Jesus invites us to *abide in His love.* We are to settle our souls down deep in His overwhelming, never-ending, covenant-keeping love and live there as humble recipients of this gift of love He came to give.

Pray Today

Dear Jesus, Thank You for loving us. We are quite often unlovable, distracted and amused by our love for worldly things, yet You never stop loving us. Teach us to abide in Your love and allow the love You have poured into us to overflow to the people You have put in our lives to love. We love You. Amen.

Day 35: The Gift Of Joy

Christianity is a divine project of replacing inferior joys in inferior objects
with superior joys in God Himself.
—John Piper[30]

John 15:11 – *These things I have spoken to you so that My joy may be in you, and that your joy may be made full.*

Jesus came to give us joy. Not just any kind of joy, but *His* joy, which is a perfect, divine, and holy joy. The world can only offer a temporary kind of happiness, which comes and goes depending on the circumstances of our days. The joy Jesus gives is a deep, abiding sense of gladness that can sustain us through the difficult times that are sure to be part of our Christian experience.

Jesus' joy is available to all who come to Him by faith, but it is conditional. A person can believe by faith and receive salvation and yet fail to walk in the joy of the Lord. Jesus gives us the secret of experiencing joy in John 15:1-11. *Stop and take a few minutes now to read these incredible verses!* There are three key words in Jesus' words to the disciples: **abide**, **obey**, and **bear fruit**.

Joy is a result of abiding.
(John 15:4,9)

To abide is to dwell, to remain or to tarry. It is used in reference both to time and place, as well as condition. Jesus commands us to dwell with Him, to spend time in His presence. We are reminded many times to "hold fast" to our faith and the Word of God, meaning a deliberate choice to continue in Christ and not be drawn away by other things. When we tarry, we wait; we give God an opportunity to meet with us. By spending time in His Word, we open our spiritual ears to listen, and allow God to open our spiritual eyes to see truth.

To abide in Christ is to live in a very real and practical awareness that He is ever-present. It is to set our minds on the Spirit, inviting Jesus into our every thought, word, and deed. As we delight ourselves in Him, we will experience real joy that surpasses all other things which masquerade as pleasure or fleeting happiness.

Psalm 37:4 – *Delight yourself in the Lord; and He will give you the desires of your heart.*

Psalm 16:11 – *You will make known to me the path of life; in Your presence is fullness of joy; in Your right hand there are pleasures forever.*

Joy is a result of obedience.
(John 15:7,10)

The result of abiding is obedience, and obedience increases our desire to abide. Disobedience to God's scriptural commands or an unwillingness to submit our lives to His will causes us to run *away* from God, the very opposite of abiding. When we learn to love His Word and surrender ourselves in obedience, we experience His abiding presence, and the joy that comes from being in right relationship with our Creator. We were made to worship God; obedience is worship made practical.

Psalm 1:2 – *But his delight is in the law of the Lord, and in His law he meditates day and night.*

Psalm 51:12 – *Restore to me the joy of Your salvation and sustain me with a willing spirit.*

Joy is a result of bearing fruit.
(John 15:4-5,8)

As we abide in Jesus, we obey Him and as a result, we bear fruit for the kingdom of God. Jesus is the vine; we are simply branches connected to (abiding in) the vine. Fruit is not a product of the branch, but the vine. God's Holy Spirit in us is the life-producing (fruit-bearing) force of the vine.

Joy is a fruit of the Spirit (Galatians 5:22), and His indwelling presence brings a continually filling with joy (Acts 13:52). The Spirit also bears fruit through answered prayer; we learn to pray according to God's will, in Jesus' name, and this brings us great joy (John 16:24).

Psalm 92:4 – *For You, O Lord, have made me glad by what You have done, I will sing for joy at the works of Your hands.*

Nothing compares to the joy we find in Jesus. Abide in Him. Obey Him completely and allow Him to produce fruit through you. Don't miss the gift of joy.

Pray Today

Dear Jesus, Thank You for the gift of joy. In a world filled with sadness, You gave us the secret to living with joy. Teach us to abide in You and enjoy Your presence. Help us to obey readily and find joy in seeing You grow the kingdom. Nothing in this world will ever make us genuinely happy; real and lasting joy is only found in You. Amen.

DAY 36: THE GIFT OF COMFORT

> I know nothing which can so comfort the soul,
> so calm the swelling billows of grief and sorrow;
> so speak peace to the winds of trial,
> as a devout musing upon the subject of the Godhead.
> –Charles Spurgeon

2 Corinthians 1:3-4 – *Blessed be the God and Father of our Lord Jesus Christ, the Father of mercies and God of all comfort, who comforts us in all our affliction so that we will be able to comfort those who are in any affliction with the comfort with which we ourselves are comforted by God.*

What comes to mind when you hear the word "comfort?" For many people, comfort is equated with the circumstances of our physical lives. We desire to live in comfortable homes. We are afraid to be "pushed out of our comfort zones." We fall asleep in comfortable beds and wake up to pursue a life of greater comforts.

This is not the kind of comfort Jesus came to give us. In the New Testament, the word *comfort* is translated from the Greek word *paraklēsis*, with a literal meaning of *to come alongside.* It is the strength and hope given to ease our grief in afflictions and trials, and it is found in the presence of Jesus. Jesus knows the human experience is filled with disappointment, hurt, and grief. He was "made like us" so that He could offer more than pity or platitudes. He has suffered, endured, and overcome. He has the knowledge and experience to comfort us no matter how deep our grieving or distress may be.

The disciples found great comfort in being with Jesus. In fact, even when they thought they might face death for their association with Him, His presence was such a comfort, they were willing to go with Him (John 11:16). Later, when the soldiers actually came with their swords and ropes and took Jesus away from them, they scattered like leaves in the wind. With Jesus gone, their comfort vanished, and they were filled with fear (Mark 14:50). Craving the comfort of His presence, only John and Peter followed Jesus into the lion's mouth of those who desired to kill Him.

Jesus had warned them He was leaving, but He promised not to leave them comfortless, as orphans. *I will ask the Father, and He will give you another Helper, that He may be with you forever* (John 14:16). "Helper" is also translated "Comforter," "Counselor," and "Advocate;" it comes from the same root word, *paraklētos.* The Holy Spirit, given to all who place their faith in Jesus, is the living source of eternal comfort in us, because He brings the presence of Jesus. Here are three ways we can experience the comfort Jesus came to give us.

The comfort of Jesus sustains us in our daily walk.
2 Thessalonians 2:16-17 – *Now may our Lord Jesus Christ Himself and God our Father, who has loved us and given us eternal comfort and good hope by grace, comfort and strengthen your hearts in every good work and word.*

Jesus comforts and strengthens us in both our work and our words. We know that we are simply vessels allowing the Holy Spirit to work in and through us, enlightening our minds to understand God's Word, and empowering us to speak words of hope and life through the gospel. Therefore, this "work and word" is both ours, and God's. Have you ever done something you thought was God's will, but it turned out terribly, and you knew you had somehow missed what God was doing? Jesus comforts us, reminding us that God is able to work all things for good when we love Him and are called to serve Him (Romans 8:28). Have you ever regretted the words that came out of your mouth? Jesus comforts us, giving us strength to apologize and assuring us that He still loves us, and will never abandon us (Romans 8:38-39). As we abide in Jesus, we work and speak for God and are comforted that His presence will lead us.

The comfort of Jesus sustains us when we face death.
Psalm 23:4 – *Even though I walk through the valley of the shadow of death, I fear no evil, for You are with me; Your rod and Your staff, they comfort me.*

Physical death is a real fear for many people, but for those who have found comfort in Jesus, death is simply a door into the presence of God. Jesus Himself stands to greet us, and I believe He is present at the death of each and every saint, comforting them as they transition from this world to the next. Jesus will not leave us at the time we need Him most. Just as a shepherd uses his rod and staff to protect and guide his flock, Jesus will hold us tightly and get us home safely.

The comfort of Jesus sustains us with the hope of eternal life.
1 Thessalonians 4:18 – *Therefore comfort one another with these words.*

Perhaps the greatest comfort we can have is the promise of eternal life. Death keeps our bodies buried until the time of their redemption, but the soul and spirit go to be with Jesus. Paul encourages us that neither we, nor our loved ones will be left in the grave. At Jesus' return, we will receive our final comfort; our mortal bodies will be changed in the twinkling of an eye and we will be clothed in immortality, to live forever in the comforting presence of Jesus.

Pray Today

Dear Jesus, Thank You for the gift of comfort. No matter how deep our griefs may be in this life, Your sustaining presence is a comfort. Teach us to run to You and not to other things which may numb our pain temporarily but can never truly bring us the comfort we crave. And as we lean on You to find our comfort, may we give comfort to those around us who are hurting; helping them to find You. Amen.

SPECTACULAR GIFTS
Day 37 – Day 40

In My Father's house are many dwelling places;
if it were not so, I would have told you; for I go to prepare a place for you.
If I go and prepare a place for you,
I will come again and receive you to Myself,
that where I am, there you may be also.
John 14:2-3

Jesus didn't come just to make this life better.
He is the ultimate long-term planner.
No short-sighted goals were in mind when He went to the cross.
Jesus came to *visit* us, but we're going home to *live* with Him.
We can't really imagine what's in store for us when we fold up our tents and
move to our permanent residence.
But it's fun to try.

DAY 37: THE GIFT OF COVENANT

Very soon the shadow will give way to Reality.
The partial will pass into the Perfect.
The foretaste will lead to the Banquet.
The troubled path will end in Paradise.
A hundred candle-lit evenings will come to their consummation
in the marriage supper of the Lamb.
And this momentary marriage will be swallowed up by Life.
Christ will be all and in all.
—John Piper[31]

Revelation 19:7-9 – *Let us rejoice and be glad and give the glory to Him, for the marriage of the Lamb has come and His bride has made herself ready. It was given to her to clothe herself in fine linen, bright and clean; for the fine linen is the righteous acts of the saints. Then he said to me, "Write, 'Blessed are those who are invited to the marriage supper of the Lamb.'" And he said to me, "These are true words of God."*

One of the pictures God gives us in scripture to describe the relationship between Himself and His people is that of a bridegroom and bride. John the Baptist referred to himself as a friend of the bridegroom, announcing Jesus as the bridegroom. Jesus taught parables about wedding feasts to illustrate the kingdom of heaven (Matthew 22:1-14; 25:1-13) and confirmed that indeed He is the bridegroom as John said (Matthew 9:14-15; Mark 2:18-20).

Paul further expanded this illustration as he taught husbands and wives how to have a godly marriage. Christ is the head of the church and loves and nurtures His bride, just as husband should love and care for his wife. The wife submits herself to the husband's authority by respecting him, just as the bride of Christ submits to Jesus.

This picture of a marriage is brought to completion in Revelation at the announcement of the marriage supper of the Lamb. All sin has been done away with, and the wicked have been judged. There is a great celebration in heaven, a celebration that Jesus and His bride are finally together for eternity.

Many people believe the Galilean wedding customs of Jesus' day are a picture of when He will return to rapture the church. A bride price is paid by the father of the groom, and a cup of wine was received to indicate the bride accepted. From that time on, they were betrothed, a covenant that was as legally binding as marriage. The groom would return to his father's house and begin preparing a home for his bride. When the father determined the house was ready, he would give his son the word, and he would go and get his bride. A marriage ceremony would take place, and the couple would withdraw to their home to consummate the marriage, after which they would celebrate with a great supper with all their friends and family.

Jesus came to give us the gift of a covenant relationship that will last throughout eternity. It is a marriage covenant between Jesus and His bride, the church, but it is also called the new covenant that He initiated and paid for by shedding His blood on the cross, making salvation possible.

Isaiah 61:10 – *I will rejoice greatly in the Lord, my soul will exult in my God; for He has clothed me with garments of salvation, He has wrapped me with a robe of righteousness, as a bridegroom decks himself with a garland, and as a bride adorns herself with her jewels.*

Do you see why God treasures marriage? Marriage between a man and woman depicts the intimate, personal and lasting relationship between Jesus and His bride. He has "paid our dowry" with His own blood (1 Peter 1:18-19); He has given us an "engagement ring" in the indwelling Holy Spirit (Ephesians 1:14), a guarantee that He will one day come for us and take us to the Father's house, where He is preparing a place for us (John 14:2-3).

Right now, we are getting ready for our wedding. Jesus is preparing His bride, *that He might present to Himself the church in all her glory, having no spot or wrinkle or any such thing; but that she would be holy and blameless* (Ephesians 5:27). Every trial, every tear, every challenge is ironing out our wrinkles and getting rid of any spots or blemishes, as His righteousness becomes more and more evident in us.

Jesus came to be bridegroom and to give us the gift of a covenant relationship that will last for eternity. What a spectacular celebration it will be.

Isaiah 62:5 – *For as a young man marries a virgin, so your sons will marry you; and as the bridegroom rejoices over the bride, so your God will rejoice over you.*

Pray Today

Dear Jesus, Thank You for the gift of covenant. You desired us, chose us, and called us. You are making us into Your image and preparing us for the great marriage celebration when we will be united with You, face to face. We can't wait for the wedding! We love You, our precious Bridegroom, and can't wait to spend all eternity with You. Amen.

DAY 38: THE GIFT OF IMMORTALITY

Some day you will read in the papers that D.L. Moody of East Northfield, is dead. Don't you believe a word of it! At that moment I shall be more alive than I am now; I shall have gone up higher, that is all, out of this old clay tenement into a house that is immortal- a body that death cannot touch, that sin cannot taint; a body fashioned like unto His glorious body.

–Dwight L. Moody

1 Corinthians 15:50-55 – *Now I say this, brethren, that flesh and blood cannot inherit the kingdom of God; nor does the perishable inherit the imperishable. Behold, I tell you a mystery; we will not all sleep, but we will all be changed, in a moment, in the twinkling of an eye, at the last trumpet; for the trumpet will sound, and the dead will be raised imperishable, and we will be changed. For this perishable must put on the imperishable, and this mortal must put on immortality. But when this perishable will have put on the imperishable, and this mortal will have put on immortality, then will come about the saying that is written, "Death is swallowed up in victory. O death, where is your victory? O death, where is your sting?"*

Did you ever stop to think about why there is such a fascination with superheroes, vampires, and mythical creatures? Books, movies, and television series are almost guaranteed success when they appeal to our innate desires for immortality. We love to think about what life would be like if we could heal ourselves, escape all the things that cause us pain, and live forever.

The desire for immortality is natural; we were created to live forever. God breathed into Adam and he became a living soul (Genesis 2:7). God's intention was for us to live eternally in His presence, choosing freely to love and worship Him in a place designed and created for our pleasure. In His sovereign plan, He chose to give Adam and Eve a choice; they could obey Him and gain eternal life immediately or disobey and bring suffering and death to all who would be born after them. They chose to sin, and fell from the perfect, immortal state in which they had been created.

Jesus came to give us back the gift of immortality that was stolen by sin. He, being God, overcame death. While He suffered in a physical body, and experienced physical death, the immortal power of God could not be held in a grave. God raised Him up, and now, in Him, we are given the gift of immortality. We will live forever.

When we take our last breath and transition from mortal to immortal, what can we expect? We only need to look at Jesus for the answers.

Our immortal bodies will be physical bodies.
Luke 24:38-39 – *And He said to them, "Why are you troubled, and why do doubts arise in your hearts? See My hands and My feet, that it is I Myself; touch Me and see, for a spirit does not have flesh and bones as you see that I have."*

Jesus appeared to many after His bodily resurrection; we can anticipate our redeemed bodies will be like His. The disciples thought they were seeing a ghost. After all, they had watched Jesus die and helped bury His body. But Jesus assured them He was just as real as they were by allowing them to touch His hands and feet. God also tells us He will "dwell among us" in heaven, indicating we will have physical bodies (Revelation 21:3).

Our immortal bodies will eat and drink.
Luke 24:42-43 – *They gave Him a piece of a broiled fish; and He took it and ate it before them.*

To completely assure the disciples He was a physical being, He ate in front of them. We will consume food in heaven as well, as Jesus promised the disciples He would again eat the Passover meal and drink the cup of the covenant with them once the kingdom of God was fulfilled (Luke 22:16,18). We also learned yesterday there will be a great marriage supper of the Lamb!

Our immortal bodies will no longer suffer corruption.
1 Peter 1:23 – *For you have been born again not of seed which is perishable but imperishable, that is, through the living and enduring word of God.*

We inherit our predisposition to sin and death from Adam, but when we are born again, we are born of *imperishable* seed, or seed that cannot be corrupted. Immortality means sickness, disease, pain, suffering, sin, or death can never touch us again. We will be forever pure and holy, healthy and whole. There are no doctors or pharmacies in heaven!

Eternal life is found in Jesus alone. Open the gift of immortality, and live.

Revelation 21:3-4 – *And I heard a loud voice from the throne, saying, "Behold, the tabernacle of God is among men, and He will dwell among them, and they shall be His people, and God Himself will be among them, and He will wipe away every tear from their eyes; and there will no longer be any death; there will no longer be any mourning, or crying, or pain; the first things have passed away.*

Pray Today

Dear Jesus, Thank You for the gift of immortality. We are able to endure the pain and suffering in this world because we anticipate the glorious redemption of our bodies to be like You. We long for the day when the curse is finally reversed, and we are walking with You in immortality. We pray for that day to come soon! Amen.

DAY 39: THE GIFT OF REWARDS

Let us remember, there is One who daily records all we do for Him,
and sees more beauty in His servants' work than His servants do themselves.
And then shall His faithful witnesses discover, to their wonder and surprise,
that there never was a word spoken on their Master's behalf,
which does not receive a reward.
–J.C. Ryle[32]

1 Corinthians 3:12-15 – *Now if any man builds on the foundation with gold, silver, precious stones, wood, hay, straw, each man's work will become evident; for the day will show it because it is to be revealed with fire, and the fire itself will test the quality of each man's work. If any man's work which he has built on it remains, he will receive a reward. If any man's work is burned up, he will suffer loss; but he himself will be saved, yet so as through fire.*

We've already seen that Jesus has promised to receive us as His bride and give us immortality; we will live eternally in His presence. That alone is enough to motivate and inspire us to be faithful to the end, but there are more gifts to open. There is a reward ceremony to attend. It's called the judgment seat of Christ and every believer will stand before Christ and give account for how we've spent our lives since we received salvation (2 Corinthians 5:10).

Because we are in Christ, our place in heaven is secure. Christ has paid our sin debt. Rather, this judgment is an awards ceremony at which we will either gain rewards to lay at Christ's feet, or be made aware of rewards lost through our disobedience or unfaithfulness during this life. We will be recompensed, or "receive back" what we've given to the Lord (Ephesians 6:7-8; Colossians 3:23-24).

What are the kinds of rewards that are waiting for us in heaven?

There are positions to fill.
Matthew 19:27-28 – *Then Peter said to Him, "Behold, we have left everything and followed You; what then will there be for us?" And Jesus said to them, "Truly I say to you, that you who have followed Me, in the regeneration when the Son of Man will sit on His glorious throne, you also shall sit upon twelve thrones, judging the twelve tribes of Israel.*

Those who give up their lives to follow Christ will receive the opportunity to reign with Him, serving the kingdom in positions of authority. Our faithfulness to the "little things" in this life will reap the reward of more responsibility in Jesus' kingdom (2 Timothy 2:12; Revelation 5:10, 20:4).

There are crowns to return.
Revelation 4:10-11 – *The twenty-four elders will fall down before Him who sits on the throne and will worship Him who lives forever and ever, and will cast their crowns before the throne, saying, "Worthy are You, our Lord and our God, to receive glory and honor and power; for You created all things, and because of Your will they existed, and were created."*

There are at least four specific crowns mentioned in the Bible that can be earned by Christ-followers: a crown of life for those who love the Lord and remain faithful during trials and suffering (James 1:12); a crown of righteousness for those who faithfully finish their course and love His appearing (2 Timothy 4:7-8); a crown of glory for those who faithfully shepherd other believers (1 Peter 5:4); and an imperishable crown for those who faithfully run the race of life (1 Corinthians 9:24-25). Notice the common thread necessary to earn these crowns: *faithfulness,* which is only possible as Christ lives out His life through us. Any crowns which we are given are rightfully placed at Jesus' feet.

There is an inheritance to receive.
Colossians 3:23-24 – *Whatever you do, do your work heartily, as for the Lord rather than for men, knowing that from the Lord you will receive the reward of the inheritance. It is the Lord Christ whom you serve.*

There are references throughout the New Testament to the promise of rewards for the faithful actions of Christ-followers. We are rewarded for endurance in suffering (Hebrews 10:34-36), experiencing persecution (Matthew 5:11-13), serving God's messengers (Mark 9:41), loving our enemies, doing good, lending without an expectation of return (Luke 6:35), and for humility and secrecy in praying, fasting and giving to the poor (Matthew 6:1-6).

These rewards are all part of the inheritance of the saints. They, too, are given to those who live by faith, serving the Lord. We do not work for specific rewards; instead, we simply strive to be faithful in every area of our lives and leave the results to Jesus.

Jesus Himself is reward enough for those who love Him. The rewards we are given in response to a faithful life are simply gifts we will return to the One who made them possible.

Revelation 22:12 – *Behold, I am coming quickly, and My reward is with Me, to render to every man according to what he has done.*

Pray Today

Dear Jesus, Thank You for the promise of rewards. By striving to be faithful to You in this life, we will have something to lay at Your feet when we worship at Your throne. All our rewards are gifts from You, to be given back to You. Amen.

Day 40: The Gift Of Heaven

My Soul, you shall swim in happiness, you shall dive in seas of inconceivable
delight by reason of your union with Christ and your delight in Him and His
delight in you! I know no better idea of Heaven than to be eternally content
with Christ and Christ to be eternally content with me! And all this will happen
within a very little time. Therefore, lay aside your cares, dismiss your fears,
murmur no more. Such a destiny awaits you that you may well be content.
–Charles Spurgeon

Philippians 3:20-21 – *For our citizenship is in heaven, from which also we
eagerly wait for a Savior, the Lord Jesus Christ; who will transform the body of our
humble state into conformity with the body of His glory, by the exertion of the
power that He has even to subject all things to Himself.*

From a secular viewpoint, heaven is a dreamy state of bliss that one hopes to
achieve. It's mocked in movies and television, depicted as a very white place
where good people go and walk around in robes. The world's view of heaven is
quite limited and unimaginative; no wonder unbelievers think it sounds rather
boring.

Scripture tells a different story, for heaven is where God lives. It exists in reality,
and it is where Jesus sits at the right hand of His Father on the throne (Hebrews
12:2). All those who have died in Christ are in God's presence (2 Corinthians 5:6-
8), although scripture seems to indicate that they will not receive their glorified
bodies until Jesus returns for the body of Christ and raptures the church (1
Thessalonians 4:16). Our immortal bodies will eat and drink, we will recognize
each other, and we will have jobs to do in serving God.

The last two chapters in the Bible are some of the most encouraging words you
will ever read if you know Jesus, as they describe the spectacular beauty that
waits for us in heaven. Here are just some of the things we will experience for
eternity.

God is preparing a new heaven and a new earth.
Revelation 21:1-2 – *Then I saw a new heaven and a new earth; for the first heaven
and the first earth passed away, and there is no longer any sea. And I saw the holy
city, new Jerusalem, coming down out of heaven from God, made ready as a bride
adorned for her husband.*

This beautiful city is described as brilliant as a crystal-clear jasper, with twelve
gates, each made of a single pearl, and twelve foundation stones made of
precious jewels. It is shaped like a cube, fifteen hundred miles long, wide, and
high. It is made of pure gold, with streets of translucent gold. There are no lights,

no sun, moon, or stars, because it is illuminated by the glory of God; it is never night. It will be filled with all nationalities, tribes, and tongues.

God is going to dwell with us in heaven.
Revelation 21:3 – *And I heard a loud voice from the throne, saying, "Behold, the tabernacle of God is among men, and He will dwell among them, and they shall be His people, and God Himself will be among them.*

There is no temple in the new heaven because God the Father and Jesus the Son are the temple (we will worship them in person). The curse of sin will be ended, and we will serve God as His bond-servants.

God will do away with all pain and suffering in heaven.
Revelation 21:4 – *And He will wipe away every tear from their eyes; and there will no longer be any death; there will no longer be any mourning, or crying, or pain; the first things have passed away.*

Everything that was touched by sin is renewed and healed. There will be perfect peace and joy in the presence of God. We will be given access to the Tree of Life, which Adam and Eve were banned from at the beginning of mankind's story; it will bear twelve kinds of fruit and its leaves will heal the nations. We will drink from the river of the water of life which flows crystal clear from the throne of God and the Lamb.

One day we will close our eyes, take our last breath on earth, and step out into eternity. For those who have received the gift of Jesus, we will open our eyes and breathe in the purest air we can imagine. Our minds will be overwhelmed by the beauty that we behold. Our hearts will beat fast in anticipation as we raise our faces to the precious Savior, Jesus. We will take His outstretched hand and run gladly into His arms as we hear Him say, "Welcome home, child. I've been waiting for you."

Jesus came to give us so much more than we can imagine. Have you received Jesus as your Savior? Don't be satisfied with a shallow faith. God wants you to enjoy all the treasures found in Jesus while you walk with Him by faith today and look forward to the glorious eternity He has planned for you tomorrow.

Pray Today

Dear Jesus, How can we express our gratitude for what You have done for us? You redeemed us, forgave us for our sins and declared us righteous. You walk with us moment by moment, providing all we need for this life. You have prepared an exciting future in a beautiful city called heaven, where we will worship You for all eternity. How grateful we are for all the treasures we find in You! May we open every gift You came to give us and live in the abundance of Your grace. Amen.

A FINAL WORD: NOW WHAT?

If you are a Christ-follower, my hope is that you have been blessed and renewed in your understanding of the wonderful gifts available through a relationship with Jesus. If you are not a believer in Jesus, the first step to experiencing all the gifts described in this devotional is to respond to His offer of salvation by grace through faith. The Bible is clear that the only way to heaven is through Jesus. Here is how you can begin a relationship with Him.

Believe that God created you for a relationship with Him (believe).
Genesis 1:27 – *God created man in His own image, in the image of God He created him; male and female He created them.*
Colossians 1:16c – *All things have been created through Him and for Him.*

Recognize that you are separated from God (admit).
Romans 3:23 - *For all have sinned and fall short of the glory of God.*

Be willing to turn from your sin (repent).
1 John 1:9 – *If we confess our sins, He is faithful and righteous to forgive us our sins and to cleanse us from all unrighteousness.*

Acknowledge that Jesus died on the cross and rose from the grave (accept).
Romans 10:9-10 – *That if you confess with your mouth Jesus as Lord, and believe in your heart that God raised Him from the dead, you will be saved; for with the heart a person believes, resulting in righteousness, and with the mouth he confesses, resulting in salvation.*

Invite Jesus into your heart and life through the Holy Spirit (receive).
John 1:12 – *But as many as received Him, to them He gave the right to become children of God, even to those who believe in His name.*

What To Pray
Dear Jesus, I recognize that I am separated from You because of my personal sin, and I need Your forgiveness. I believe that You died on the cross to pay the penalty for my sin. I confess my sin and ask You to forgive me. By faith, I turn from my way of life to follow You and accept Your gift of salvation by grace. I ask You to come into my life and transform me. Thank You for saving me and giving me eternal life. In Jesus' Name, Amen.

If you sincerely prayed this prayer and surrendered your life to God, you are now His child. Please share this decision with another believer and ask him or her to help you get started in how to walk in your new life in Christ. We would love to hear about your decision!

ENDNOTES

1. John MacArthur, *MacArthur Commentary, 2 Corinthians*, Moody Press 2003, p. 198.

2. John Piper, *Faith Alone and the Fight for Joy* taken from *When the Darkness Will Not Lift*, 2006, Crossway Books. p. 16.

3. A.W. Pink, *The Sovereignty of God*, p. 79.

4. Quoted in *Putting Amazing Back into Grace* by Michael Scott Horton, Baker, 1991, p. 158.

5. John MacArthur, *Strange Fire*, 2013, p. 188.

6. Max Lucado, *Just Like Jesus.*

7. John Calvin, *Calvin's Commentary* on 1 Corinthians 1:30, Volume XX, Baker, 1993, p. 93.

8. A.W. Tozer, *How To Be Filled With The Holy Spirit.*

9. Martin Luther, *The Early Years, Christian History*, p. 34.

10. Thomas Watson, *A Puritan Golden Treasury*, compiled by I.D.E. Thomas, by permission of Banner of Truth, Carlisle, PA. 2000, p. 111.

11. Warren W. Wiersbe, *Be Wise (1 Corinthians)*, S.P. Publications, 1986, p. 38.

12. Nancy Leigh DeMoss, *Biblical Womanhood in the Home*, Crossway, 2002, p. 67.

13. Jerry Bridges, *Transforming Grace*, NavPress, 1991, p. 102.

14. John Piper, https://www.desiringgod.org/messages/my-abandoned-life-for-your-abundant-life--2.

15. J.I. Packer, *The Puritan Idea of Communion with God, in Puritan Papers, Volume 2*, 1960-1962, P&R, 2001, p. 114-115.

16. John MacArthur, *MacArthur Commentary, Ephesians*, Moody Publishers, 1986, p. 46.

17. John MacArthur, *The Master's Plan for the Church*, Moody, 1991, p. 165.

18. David Platt.

19. Daniel Cawdray, *A Puritan Golden Treasury*, compiled by I.D.E. Thomas, by permission of Banner of Truth, Carlisle, PA. 2000, p. 127.

20. Jerry Bridges, *Transforming Grace,* NavPress, 1991, p. 144.

21. Watchman Nee, *The Normal Christian Life*, Hendrickson Publishers, p. 110.

22. https://www.medicalnewstoday.com/articles/319151#how-does-muscle-grow-in-the-body.

23. www.blueletterbible.org.

24. Unknown Author, *The Kneeling Christian,* circa 1930.

25. Randy Alcorn, *The Treasure Principle*, 2002, p. 73.

26. Charles Spurgeon, *Treasury of David,* Commentary for Psalm 4:8.

27. John MacArthur, *MacArthur Commentary, 1 and 2 Thessalonians*, Moody, 2002, p. 313.

28. Victor Shepherd, *You Asked for a Sermon on Hope*, March 1999, victorshepherd.on.ca.

29. A.W. Pink, *The Attributes of God*, Baker Book House, p. 81.

30. John Piper, *Why I Love the Apostle Paul*, p. 162.

31. John Piper, *This Momentary Marriage – A Parable of Permanence, Desiring God Foundation*, 2008, p.178.

32. J. C. Ryle, *Commentary*, Matthew 11.

Where quotes are not footnoted, they are considered part of the public domain and no specific source is known. Credit to the website gracequotes.org for many of the quotes referenced.

ADDITIONAL RESOURCES

Be Strategic With The Gospel

Going Around The Corner Bible Study
ISBN: 9780692781999 / List Price: $12.99
This six-session workbook helps believers explore the mission field in their own neighborhoods and workplaces. Learn to engage others through prayer and biblical good works guided by the prompts of the Holy Spirit. Gain confidence to evangelize through sharing the complete gospel and your own story. Discover how to establish and equip new believers in their faith journey. A simple, practical, and biblical strategy for disciple-making.

Going Around The Corner Bible Study, Student Edition
ISBN: 9780692781999 / List Price: $10.99
A five-session workbook developed for high school and college students. Covers the first four chapters of the adult study with expanded commentary and application focused on reaching their campus, dorm, and playing field for Christ. Students will be guided into God's Word and develop an awareness and passion for sharing the gospel.

Going Around The Corner Bible Study, Leader Guide
ISBN: 9780999131824 / List Price: $3.99
Key truths, discussion starters and thoughtful questions to facilitate group study, plus suggested activities, and practical application steps.

Going Around The Corner: The Guidebook
ISBN: 9781733047821 / List Price: $6.99
This little guidebook helps you take what you know about the gospel and share it. Take one step at a time and implement it. Soon you will love the people God has put in your life with Christ's love, and will be interceding on their behalf. You will get to know them personally and be involved in their lives. You will be confident in sharing your own conversion story and the complete gospel. You will be the one to introduce them to Jesus.

Be Aware Of The Gospel

40 Days of Spiritual Awareness
ISBN: 9780999131800 / List Price: $9.99
Understand who God is and how He is working in the people right around you. Discover truth that will increase your awareness of God, yourself, other believers, and unbelievers. Be reminded of God's work in our world, as He redeems and saves. At the end of the 40-day journey, you will realize that you are an important part of accomplishing that work and be prepared to join Him.

Be Refreshed In The Gospel

Grace & Glory: A 50-Day Journey In The Purpose & Plan Of God
ISBN: 9780999131848 / List Price $11.99
What do we do when we face a crisis of faith? When everything we believe is challenged? That's when we must discover (or re-discover) God's purpose for our lives and learn to live with a mindset of His grace...grace that reveals His glory. This devotional will refresh believers in the gospel and encourage them to live every day so that the glory of God will be proclaimed by the power of grace at work in their lives.

Pray The Gospel

Just Pray: God's Not Done With You
ISBN: 9780999131886 / List Price $9.99

How often have you heard someone say, "All I can do is 'just pray'!" The reality is, the most powerful and effective thing we can do is pray. You are strategically, sovereignly positioned to have kingdom impact in this generation through a simple commitment to prayer. God is not looking for people of strength and confidence. He is seeking those who know they are helpless and weak so that His strength and glory can be made magnified in them. No matter what your limitations, God still has work for you to do for the kingdom. We invite you to accept the challenge and just pray.

Run With The Gospel

Let Us Run The Race
ISBN: 9781733047807 / List Price $9.99

The greatest missionary of all time, Paul made an unforgettable and enduring impact on the culture that surrounded him. If we could sit down and chat with him, what would he tell us? What can we learn from a man who ran his race so well? We all want our lives count for something greater than ourselves. The reality is, there is no greater call than the cause of Christ and the gospel of His kingdom. Let's pursue Him with passion, endurance, and joy. Let's run the race, for Jesus is worthy.

Give The Gift Of The Gospel

Living In Light of the Manger
ISBN: 9780999131817 / List Price $9.99

If the manger only has meaning during our holiday celebrations, we've missed the point of the story. Jesus was born, so that we could be *born again*. The events of His birth and the people who welcomed Him have many lessons to teach us about the glorious gospel and how Jesus came to change our lives. Discover the purpose and power of the manger. Perfect as a gift to introduce the gospel to friends, co-workers, and neighbors.

Make Disciples Of The Gospel

One-To-One Discipleship
ISBN: MM121 / List Price $17.00

A nine-session course for one believer to establish a new believer in the Christian faith, covering nine foundational stones upon which to build the new life in Christ. The biblical foundations of Assurance, Attributes of God, the Bible, Prayer, Spirit-Filled Life, Witnessing, Temptation, and Obedience contribute to a solid beginning for a new believer. Published by Multiplication Ministries and available from ATCM. A women's edition is also available. Used worldwide, this resource has sold over a million copies since it was written.

All resources are available on our website.
www.AroundTheCornerMinistries.org.

ABOUT THE AUTHOR

Sheila Alewine came to Christ at an early age, growing up in a Baptist church in Western North Carolina. She spent a lot of time in and around church with her mom who worked as the church secretary, so marrying a full-time minister came naturally. She met her husband, Todd, while attending Liberty University in Lynchburg, VA. They married in 1985 and have spent their lives serving God together while raising two daughters.

As a young mom, Sheila fell in love with Bible study when asked to join a Precept study. Throughout the years of raising their daughters, working full-time, and serving in ministry, she has loved studying and teaching in the Word. She writes for two reasons: to encourage those who know Jesus to serve Him passionately and tell others about Him, and to invite those who do not yet believe to consider Christ.

Sheila and her husband reside in Hendersonville, NC, where they have established *Around The Corner Ministries* to equip and encourage followers of Christ to share the gospel where they live, work and play. They love spending time with their daughters, sons-in-law, and grandchildren.

Connect with Sheila at her blog *https://sheilaalewine.com/*.

CONTACT US

If this devotional has made an impact on your life, please let us know by contacting us through our website **aroundthecornerministries.org**, by email to sheila@aroundthecornerministries.org, or through our Facebook page.

Around The Corner Ministries exists to take the gospel to every neighborhood in America. Our mission is to equip followers of Jesus to engage their neighborhoods and communities with the gospel of Jesus Christ.

Around The Corner Ministries is a partner to the local church, designed to teach and train Christ-followers how to evangelize their neighborhoods, workplaces, and communities. The goal is to grow healthy local churches filled with mature believers who are comfortable and passionate about sharing their faith. If you would like more information on how our ministry can partner with your local church, please contact us.

CPSIA information can be obtained
at www.ICGtesting.com
Printed in the USA
LVHW021651270521
688666LV00036B/1506